Simply Scratch

Simply Scratch

120 WHOLESOME HOMEMADE RECIPES MADE EASY

Laurie McNamara

AVERY

an imprint of Penguin Random House

New York

an imprint of Penguin Random House LLC
375 Hudson Street
New York, New York 10014

Most Avery books are available at special quantity discounts for bulk purchase for sales promotions, premiums,
fund-raising, and educational needs. Special books or book excerpts also can be created to fit specific needs.
For details, write SpecialMarkets@penguinrandomhouse.com.

Library of Congress Cataloging-in-Publication Data

McNamara, Laurie.
Simply scratch : 120 wholesome homemade recipes made easy / Laurie McNamara.
p.   cm.
ISBN 978-1-58333-579-6
1. Cooking.   2. Cooking—Anecdotes.   I. Title.
TX714.M39   2015   2015025457
641.5—dc23

Printed in the United States of America

1   3   5   7   9   10   8   6   4   2

Book design by Gretchen Achilles

To my beautiful daughters, Haileigh and Malloree:
You two are what inspires and motivates me daily.
Always remember to be brave enough to take a leap of faith and follow your dreams.
You are my everything.

And to my husband, Pat: Thank you for your continuous love and support
over these many years. For being ever so patient while waiting for me to snap
"one last picture" before we eat, and always, *always*
making me laugh. I love you.

Contents

Acknowledgments

If there's one thing that I know for certain, it's that I wouldn't have fallen madly in love with cooking if it wasn't for you, Mom. Thank you for allowing me to pull up the step stool as a kid to watch you work your culinary magic in the kitchen, for making me "try" new foods (even if I wasn't too thrilled at the time), and always sharing your wisdom, free of charge. You are a huge inspiration behind this book and the reason why I love cooking from scratch. Dad, thank you for showing me that hard work pays off, how to plant and weed a garden, and for calling me first with all your cooking questions. You *do* call me first, right?

My (more than just) in-laws, Pat and Brenda, you are amazing second parents to me. Since I was fourteen years old, you've welcomed me into your family with open arms and continue to play a huge role in my life. Brenda, it seems like yesterday we were sitting at your kitchen counter discussing this "crazy idea" of me starting a food blog and now look! Thank you for the endless cups of coffee, love and encouragement, and for teaching me that if I face my fears today, tomorrow I'll look back and wonder what was so darn scary. You both are one-of-a-kind in-laws, and I'm so lucky to have you in my life and in my corner.

My beautiful sisters, Kelly, Christine, and Julie, you girls are such a blessing, and our bond never ceases to amaze me. I wouldn't be here if it wasn't for your love and support and your ability to make me laugh and cry at the same time. Thank you for taking the time to test so many of these recipes (sometimes more than once) and for your helpful suggestions and tips. I am forever grateful to you three.

My *bestest* of friends, Nichole, Heidi, and Stacey. A huge thanks to you gals for testing recipes, sending encouraging texts, giving hugs, wiping tears, and for getting me out of the house just when I needed it most. I cherish each one of you and our many years of friendship.

This book wouldn't have even been possible without my agent and friend, Michael Sterling. Thank you for finding me among a huge sea of talented bloggers. Knowing you believe in me and this book with so much enthusiasm, plus always saying the right words of encouragement at the right time to keep me going, is appreciated more than you could possibly know. You truly are one of a kind. Lucia Watson, my brilliant editor; Gigi Campo; and the whole team at Avery that has had a hand in shaping and bringing this beautiful book to life, thank you for instantly understanding my vision and making one of my biggest dreams come true.

Last, but definitely not least, thank you from the bottom of my heart to all the *Simply Scratch* blog readers out there—those of you who take the time to read my sometimes wordy ramblings, make my recipes, leave comments, and send encouraging and heartfelt e-mails. I definitely wouldn't be here without each and every single one of you. This book is for you.

Introduction

It all started thirtysomething years ago. I grew up in Ortonville, Michigan, a small rural town in the northern part of Oakland County. Imagine your left hand is the state of Michigan; if you were to hold it up in front of you, Ortonville would be an inch over from where the crook of your thumb and first finger meet. Ortonville was (and still is) primarily made up of dirt roads, farms, and a quaint little downtown with that small-community feel. When I was a girl, there were no major shopping malls or fast-food chains, not unless you count the A&W drive-in and the Frosty Boy where we'd get ice cream after T-ball games. The lone family restaurant in town had the absolute *best* breadsticks and kiddy cocktails ever. Next to that, there was a small grocery store. Ortonville, Michigan—it was a small town.

My parents packed up and moved from the city so they could build a beautiful two-story home on a two-acre lot. It was the perfect place to raise a family; there was plenty of space for us kids to run wild, the horses had a small pasture to roam, and we grew a beautiful garden. Our property was complete with a horse corral and a tack room, which held the hay, feed, bridles, and essential grooming gear. The tack room floor was scattered with hay, and my sisters and I spent many afternoons playing there. These days, I can't breathe in the smell of hay and not think of that place and the countless hours I spent playing in it as a young girl.

Growing up on a farm meant my family had access to the freshest foods and produce. This was one of the many perks of living where I did. Rather than buying eggs at the local market, we had only to stroll out to the chicken coop to collect fresh ones. It's easy, if not tempting, however, to think that collecting fresh eggs from chickens is a leisurely activity—movies would have you believe that all you need to do is lift up the roof of a chicken coop and take a freshly laid egg straight from a plump hen's nest. Actually, it's quite the opposite: my family kept a rooster, and we had a deeply rooted fear of him and tried to dodge his attacks while we collected eggs. He'd come after you in a heartbeat. Thankfully, I was too young to collect the chicken eggs; my oldest two sisters had the unlucky responsibility of handling that job. I remember a particular time when they escaped from his clutches, bleeding. I never envied them this chore. That said, I've never tasted better eggs in my life.

One of the greatest treasures from my childhood was our family garden. I spent many summer days wandering through the rows of vegetables, fruits, and flowers. I recall my parents planting rows of corn, russet potatoes, green beans, peas, carrots, and tomatoes, but my absolute favorite parts of the garden were the strawberry patch and raspberry bush. When I was a kid, you'd find me outside at all times riding my bike, catching frogs, and snatching a berry or three (or five) while on my way to our rickety metal swing set. Every once in a while—if we were lucky—my parents would allow my sisters and me to pull a carrot straight from the soil to eat fresh. We'd rinse it off with the garden hose and plop down on the deck steps to eat our prize. Of my many wonderful memories, these moments are among my favorites.

When I was indoors, I was keenly aware of all the smells coming from our kitchen. My mom's cooking was magical, to say the least—she knew how to make three unbelievably delicious meals a day for a large family, sourcing most of the ingredients straight from our backyard or nearby co-op.

I loved coming home after a day at school to discover we were having baked chicken for dinner that night. I could smell it just moments before entering the house: the wafting scent of spices and baking chicken would linger outside our front door. It was a comforting smell. Some of my earliest food-obsessed memories start at my mother's counter. I'd pull up the rusty brown step stool to watch her hands while she kneaded pizza dough, frosted a cake, or stirred a pot of sloppy joe sauce. I can still remember the feeling of the nonslip, sandpaperlike grit under my bare feet while I "helped" my mom in the kitchen. Even today, her pizza remains one of my favorite dishes: just like when I was growing up, she makes it with a deep golden crust and the perfect smattering of toppings and cheese. She always wore her deep blue and goldenrod-trimmed floral apron, which she recently passed down to me, and never failed to turn out the perfect pizza.

If we were lucky, a homemade dessert would find its way onto the table at the end of a meal. (My fingers were permanently crossed for her Mississippi Mud Pie—you can find the recipe on page 285.) The irony of it all, however, is that I was such a picky eater—I was the child who hated cooked vegetables; spices always felt too strong on my tongue; baked potatoes induced gag reflexes in my throat (I'd even hide whole bites of it in my milk glass and just eat the pats of butter instead); and tomatoes, which in my young mind were sour tasting, would always remain around the edge of my salad bowl. If my mom wasn't home to cook a meal, that would put my dad on dinner duty. And boy, did I put him through the wringer (I knew better than to give my mom a hard time), whining about how I didn't want whatever it was he was making for dinner that night, begging him to just make me a peanut butter and jelly sandwich instead—because, truthfully, I could have eaten those every single day. I still could, actually. . . .

As I grew older, I became less picky. Trying new foods like cheesecake for the first time were big moments for me. I'd always been too stubborn to try it because, as a kid, I couldn't begin to comprehend what kind of cake could possibly taste good with *cheese* in it. (I could kick myself for the years I wasted refusing to try it!) I've requested cheesecake for every birthday or gathering since that first fateful bite. Guacamole was another one: it was green; therefore, for a long time I thought it was gross. But once I dragged a crisp, salty chip through it and took a bite, I was sold—now my family eats guacamole or avocado dip at least twice a week (even my husband loves it, and he was a guacamole hater until he met me).

So, as my palate and I both matured, my desire to cook and explore my family's cooking traditions grew, too. I fell in love with the feel of chopping vegetables, the sound of sauce simmering, and the sense of triumph as I'd pull a homemade cake out of the oven. I'd be doubly happy (or impressed with myself!) if the cake was delicious and moist.

In high school, at age fourteen, I met Pat, my future husband. Like me, he is one of the pickiest eaters I've ever known. He's pickier than I ever was, if that's even possible. To this day, if a recipe gets a thumbs-up review from him, I know it's a hit and I not-so-secretly jump for joy.

In my early twenties, I found I'd lost sight of my roots when it came to food. I was a young wife and mother working a full-time job and raising two little girls. I wanted to provide my family with substantial meals, reminiscent of the ones my mother would prepare when I was growing up. I did my best to achieve this, despite how difficult it was to regularly cook three fresh meals a day. Like most American families, I relied on boxed meal substitute, canned soups, processed foods, boxed baking mixes—the list goes on and on. It was only a short time ago that I had a bit of a revelation, though. One day, while I was reaching into my pantry for a box of brownie mix, a simple life-changing thought dawned on me: *This is not how my mom used to do it.* It was a visceral moment. I felt disappointed that I was not cooking healthier meals, that I was letting my girls eat hyperprocessed foods as frequently as, if not more often than, fresh fruits and vegetables. I remember asking myself right then, *When did it become the norm that brownies come from a box?* Then more questions reverberated through my head as I looked at my pantry: *How is it that canned soup is the only way to make a dish creamy and luscious? And does spaghetti sauce have to come from a jar, or is there another way?* My mother used to grind her own wheat into flour in our pantry, and there I was making brownies from a mix.

Then an idea flooded through me: I knew right then and there that I needed to find a way to make these things, everything, from scratch, just as my mother had. I made a pact with myself to do this, and while I knew I didn't have all day to prepare our meals—heck, I was a mom and I worked a full-time job—I was determined to find a way to eliminate as many boxed, canned, and prepackaged mixes and ingredients from my kitchen as possible. I was going to reinvent the term "from scratch" and make my kitchen into one just like my family had when I was growing up.

As the years rolled on, I attempted all kinds of recipes, including ones for household basics such as breads, barbecue sauce, mayonnaise, and ketchup. I adapted some of my mother's treasured classic recipes for my own kitchen, and I dreamed up new ones to share with my girls. I took inspiration from cookbooks and restaurants or from meals with friends and family for new dishes or techniques I'd never tried before. I wrote all my successful recipes down in a red composition notebook, and my collection grew rapidly over time. My goal was to develop strategies to maintain a purely from-scratch kitchen, so that our family could eat affordably, conveniently, and more healthfully. Slowly but surely, I successfully removed all hyperprocessed foods from my kitchen. In early 2010, I started my blog, *Simply Scratch*, to chronicle my from-scratch adventure and share it with friends and family. I quickly realized that people were shocked (impressed?) not only that I was attempting to cook exclusively from scratch, but that I was succeeding. I wanted to show them just how easy a whole-food, from-scratch lifestyle was, and the result has been incredible. *Simply Scratch* has walked thousands of home cooks—moms and dads, novice and experienced home chefs, and foodies—step-by-step through my favorite from-scratch recipes. With hundreds of recipes in my archive, my blog has become a go-to resource for home cooks as they plan their meals throughout the week. My blog is my creative outlet, my passion. It humbles me to be connected with readers around the world who write to share their success at making their first recipe from scratch or from those looking for healthier alternatives to avoid additives in prepackaged or canned ingredients. With the success of my blog, I was able to quit my full-time job to blog exclusively, and I've never looked back. It's a dream come true to be writing this book and to share with you the recipes I hold near and dear.

I've always believed food forms the bonds that make our memories and family connections. It's very important to me that we all sit down for dinner every night and that Sundays are our family breakfast day. My favorite thing in the world is having my girls help me cook in the kitchen just like I used to help my mom. I find inspiration in everything around me, from seasonal fruits, vegetables, and the herbs that grow in my garden, to dishes I've had at restaurants that I simply *have* to make at home because they were so delicious. Basically, I like to cook the meals that I like to eat (who doesn't, right?), and this book is a reflection of that.

In the beginning of this cookbook you will find recipes for simple pantry basics such as mayo, ketchup, starches, and sauces, items that we all typically buy every week. You'll have the option to make these from scratch and to use them throughout the recipes that follow. You can't go wrong with any of these DIY basics. They're simple, approachable, and without a doubt delicious. To those who fear cooking from scratch is too challenging, I promise you that once you nail down the basics and properly stock your pantry, you'll soon realize that making homemade meals can become as second nature as breathing. Just take your first step. Soon you'll be high-fiving yourself after a darn good 100 percent from-scratch meal!

Since that fateful day with the brownie mix, it has always been my goal to use fresh, healthy ingredients and to cook from scratch. I hope you enjoy the many scrumptious recipes in this book, as they are tried and true, from my kitchen to yours.

—LAURIE

Simply Scratch

CHAPTER ONE

Basics

The Scratch Pantry

My pantry wasn't always a *scratch pantry*. If we were to teleport back in time to just six years ago and land smack-dab in the center of my old kitchen, my cooking—and my life—would be in stark contrast to what it is today. First, it would literally be a different kitchen, since we moved a few years ago. But you'd also see clearly that I seriously lacked confidence as a home cook.

My old, white-veneered, plywood pantry cabinet was a very well-loved and well-used treasure from Target, but it also was a mess. It was stuffed, in no order, with cans of cream-of-whatever soup, jars of premade pasta sauce, baking supplies, not to mention several opened bags of chocolate chips crammed into ziplock baggies (to satisfy my occasional craving for a spoonful of peanut butter topped with chocolate chips). There was also a basket filled with jarred herbs, spices and spice blends, boxes of macaroni and cheese, eight different kinds of cereal, and usually a box of brownie mix. Okay, so maybe two boxes, *plus* a tub of frosting. I cringe. My husband once used the term "food hoarder" to describe me, and while I try not to say this *too* often, he was completely right.

Today, I would proudly show you my pantry and cupboards: they're tidy and organized, and over the years they've been transformed into well-stocked shelves with crucial from-scratch cooking necessities. No canned soups, boxed mixes, or jars of sauce. (I've even got a shelf dedicated to lots of different vinegars. Some habits are hard to break, and buying infused vinegars is a weakness of mine. . . .)

But it took a while to get from point A to point B. When I decided to start cooking exclusively from scratch, I faced a frustratingly simple (but terrifying) question: *Where do I even begin?* I vividly remember looking around at my kitchen while trying to decide what to do first. *Should I toss the Cheez-Its and frostings and cake mixes, and empty every square inch of my cupboard? Or should I just eat everything in sight so I'm not wasting all that money by throwing everything in the trash? Do I need to go to Bed Bath & Beyond and purchase every pot, pan, and kitchen tool known to man?* It seemed pretty daunting, even overwhelming, and I was suddenly regretting never having a wedding shower. . . .

Right down to my cooking tools, I literally had to start from scratch.

But here's the best advice I learned to keep in mind as you get started: you don't have to make the transition all at once, but once you make the decision, begin making changes at your very next trip to the grocery store. Why wait? Transforming your kitchen to a from-scratch kitchen can be as easy as setting a goal to make one from-scratch recipe per week; just buy the ingredients (and any special tool you'll need) and from there you can slowly work your way up to more recipes. In the process, you'll build your scratch pantry and stock of kitchen tools, and gain the confidence to cook the basics and then the more complex recipes. Oh, and your skills at dicing and chopping will vastly improve. Going slowly is crucial to not getting overwhelmed and quitting. Trust me—it's that simple.

Pantry and Fridge Essentials

Once you are on your way, having a properly stocked kitchen is essential to making cooking from scratch a joy and a breeze (and not a frustrating endeavor). Below is a list of staple ingredients I always keep on hand in my scratch pantry. I'm not too picky: I don't buy the fanciest, most expensive brands (unless it's absolutely necessary). The bottom line is I do my best with what I can find and afford—you don't need organic this or certified that to cook from scratch. As long as you have a properly stocked pantry with the basic ingredients, you can pretty much make just about anything from scratch!

At one point in my life I had seven—count 'em—*seven* bags of flour in my cupboard. I kept unbleached all-purpose flour, whole wheat flour, whole wheat white flour, bread flour, self-rising flour, buckwheat flour, and cake flour. Yikes. (Looking back, I shudder.) I have since narrowed it down a smidge to three: unbleached, whole wheat, and buckwheat flour. If I ever need a different one, I'll just pick it up at the store when a recipe calls for it.

A note on storing flour: Once you open a bag of flour, the shelf life decreases, so if you aren't using flour regularly, a great way to keep flour fresh is to pour it into a freezer-safe container and store it in your freezer. Avoid storing flour in its original packaging because the paper bag is porous. The flour can absorb flavors from the freezer, or even the smell of the bag itself. (Yes, I learned this lesson the hard way.) I use whole wheat and buckwheat flours less frequently, so you'd most definitely find those in my freezer to keep them fresh longer.

FATS, OILS, AND APPLESAUCE

I'm pretty darn particular about which fats and oils I use to cook in my kitchen. It's probably the only thing I would say I have strong feelings about (in fact, I have to try my best not to preach about it too much). It's an ongoing joke in our house that we may run out of bread, but we always, *always* have butter. Darn right.

BACON FAT

One of my favorite things to talk about is bacon fat. It's an extremely versatile fat to keep on hand. I use it to grease pans for baked goods, sauté vegetables, fry eggs; really, the options are endless. I have two jars (no joke) in my fridge. The "refined" jar is bacon fat that I pour from the pan through a mesh strainer into a glass jar. This is a great substitute for butter when you want to kick up the flavor, and I use strained bacon fat for greasing baking dishes, brushing on corn on the cob before I grill it—seriously, try it—and for many other uses. The "unstrained" jar is unstrained bacon fat that I use for frying eggs, sautéing vegetables (for sauces, chilis, stews, etc.) or for popping popcorn. It's purely a personal preference to use unstrained or strained bacon fat in cooking—you can never go wrong using either.

BUTTER

I keep my fridge stocked with both salted and unsalted butter. I use salted butter for spreading on bread or toast, or a pat on my baked potato. Unsalted butter is better for cooking and baking because you have more control of the salt content in your dishes and baked goods. In both the sweet and savory recipes here in the book, I use unsalted butter (unless otherwise noted).

LARD

I primarily use lard for searing large pieces of meat before braising or roasting. I also use it in my rolled dumplings, and it adds great flavor when making Skillet Refried Black Beans (page 195). I probably use it the least of all the fats listed here, but with its long shelf life, I always have it on hand for whenever I need it.

OILS

As far as oils go, I strictly use olive oil, grape-seed, coconut, peanut, sunflower, safflower, and sesame oils. I love safflower, coconut, and grape-seed oils for roasting and pan-frying, and olive oil for making salad dressings. I also use coconut oil for cooking pancakes, French toast, and in baked goods. For stir-frying, I prefer to use sesame, sunflower, safflower, and peanut oils, since their smoking points are high (450°F or higher) and they can handle serious heat.

I'd like to shine a spotlight on grape-seed oil, if I may. It's a multitasking oil. It's great for making homemade mayo (page 25) and peanut butter (you can find that recipe on my website), for example. You can also substitute it in virtually any baking recipe that calls for oil. I truly love this stuff. If you're shopping on a budget, I'd recommend you buy grape-seed, safflower, and olive oils, if you had to pick just a few. You can easily get by with these.

I'm personally not a fan of vegetable or canola oils, which usually are highly processed and treated.

APPLESAUCE

I know what you're thinking: applesauce wouldn't typically be found in the oil section of your grocery store (or other cookbooks!) *but* it's a great healthy alternative to oil in baked goods. I buy all natural, unsweetened applesauce and swap oil for applesauce in equal measures in recipes. It has always made me cringe to pour a cup of oil into a batter, so applesauce is my favorite healthy way to cut back on oil in a recipe. I especially love it in my Olive Oil Zucchini Bread (page 288).

DRIED HERBS AND SPICES

If I were to open my spice drawer and count all the jars of herbs and spices, the total number would be a staggering eighty jars. (And yes, I did just go and count them.) I'm a crazy person when it comes to making my own spice mixes and seasoning blends (see page 36), so I keep many herbs and spices on hand to avoid buying packets in the grocery store. If kept in an airtight container in a cool, dark place, ground spices can last from six to twelve months before they start losing their potency, whole spices and dried green leafy herbs for one to two years, and seeds for roughly three to four years. I'm like a revolving door when it comes to spices, and I rarely have to toss out any expired jars . . . which saves me lots of money.

If I *had* to pick only a handful of spices that I use most often, though, it would be pretty tough. But my top five would be basil, oregano, paprika, cumin, and red pepper flakes. Oh, and chili powder—both ancho and regular—and vanilla and cardamom. Oops, that's nine. Oh well. Having these spices on hand at all times will help keep your cooking versatile, fun, and delicious, and you'll be able to tackle virtually any recipe.

My favorite spice brand is Simply Organic. I love the quality and strong flavor of their spices and herbs. As an added bonus, the lids of their crystal-clear jars are labeled with the name of the spice or herb on top, which helps me locate the jar I need much more quickly. For larger quantities and/or harder to find spices, I go to Penzeys, where I can find spices and herbs like lavender, sumac, Aleppo pepper, and fancy kinds of black pepper, to name a few.

In the summer months, I keep a raised garden off my front porch. I grow my own rosemary, thyme, chives, basil, and oregano. I cook with herbs from these plants all summer long, and it's a sad day when fall rolls into winter and I have to pack it in. During winter months, you'll always find fresh flat-leaf parsley and cilantro in my fridge—I buy these from the grocery store. They add a boost of freshness, a pop of color, and a distinct herbaceousness that finishes off a dish nicely. If I need any other fresh herbs, I pick them up at the grocery store on an as-needed basis.

SALT AND PEPPER

I keep several types of salt in my pantry, mainly kosher salt, table salt, and sea salt. Lots of people have asked me, *What is kosher salt and how is it different from table salt?* The simplest, nonscientific answer I have is that kosher salt grains are larger and flatter than table salt. You use less because of this size, and when it's sprinkled on a hunk of meat (along with its BFF, black pepper), it will form a *great* crust. I also personally think kosher salt has a more subtle taste than regular old table salt. It's great in salad dressings, for baking, margarita making (truth!), and seasoning vegetables while they sauté in a pan.

I especially love large flaked sea salt for finishing a dish or sprinkling on warm, freshly baked chocolate chip cookies. I also keep fine sea salt around for making my recipe for All-Purpose Seasoned Salt (page 38). Of course, I have pink Himalayan salt, smoked sea salt, and truffle salt—but those are just extra-fancy ones that you really don't need . . . they're just fun to buy. Sorry, Pat!

VINEGARS

I love buying vinegars like most girls like buying purses or shoes. It's a fact that I have a shelf dedicated to vinegars. I make salad dressing and marinades so often that I love to switch it up by using different vinegars like pear or cabernet vinegar. But as a rule I always have balsamic vinegar, white wine vinegar, regular distilled vinegar, apple cider vinegar, and red wine vinegar on hand at all times. When you are making salad dressings or marinades, you can use almost any vinegar—I fully encourage you to explore and have fun! Just keep the measurements the same, and go for it!

These add flavor and much needed texture to things like salads, cookies, and poultry and fish when crusted with them. I keep almonds, pecans, walnuts, and pine nuts on hand all the time. Always—*always*—store any and all nuts in the fridge. They have delicate oils in them that can become rancid over time if they're not stored properly. Ever taste a walnut gone bad? Well, it's not good.

I also have sesame, poppy, pepitas, ground flax, and shelled sunflower seeds, and I keep them stored in separate airtight containers in a cool, dark place. One tasty way to enjoy seeds in dishes is to toast them. To do this, heat them in a dry skillet over medium-low heat until fragrant.

CITRUS

Basically, I'm talking about lemons and limes here, and on occasion oranges. Citrus adds a touch of acidity to salad dressings, acts as a tenderizer in marinades, and can brighten up an overly rich or overly flat dish. I also love to use their zest in baked goods or to make my own citrus salt blends. A squeeze of lime over Broiled Chili-Lime-Crusted Tilapia (page 249) is where it's at. I always keep a lemon or two in my fridge; they can last for a while and are extremely useful.

ONIONS & GARLIC

Onions and garlic are key ingredients for adding flavor when you cook from scratch. Nine times out of ten, a savory recipe will call for one, if not both of them. My grocery store carries a mixed bag of onions that I like to buy: it has a few yellow, white, and red onions, so this makes it easy to always have variety, and I don't end up with too much of any one kind.

I always keep fresh garlic on hand, too. I buy it from the bulk bin and try to stay away from the ones in the mesh sleeves. My experience is they sprout off easier and the cloves are always *so* tiny. Also, in my opinion jarred garlic does not taste the same as fresh garlic. As tempting as it is to buy the jarred variety to save yourself from having to mince—and more important, to keep your fingers from smelling like raw garlic—I strongly urge you to buy fresh, firm bulbs with tight skins and skip right on past the jar. You won't regret it.

Kitchen Tools & Equipment

Like most people, I slowly built my kitchen one tool and appliance at a time. It started in my early twenties when I received a blender as a baby shower gift so I could make my own baby food for my first daughter. Then, later on, my sister Julie bought me my very first *real* chef's knife and cutting board, and that helped grow my passion for cooking. I think— and I'm not sure *why*—most people might be upset to receive a kitchen tool or gadget as a gift from a spouse for their birthday or a holiday. I'm *so* not that person; I don't ask for anything else. Over the many years my husband and I have been together, Pat has bought me more treasured kitchen gifts than I can count, from my very first food processor to my Kitchen-Aid stand mixer. Here are some of my favorite tools. All of these will go a long way toward helping you keep a from-scratch kitchen with ease.

GARLIC PRESS

To say I am in love with my garlic press could possibly be a little embarrassing, but I *so* totally am. Not only does it get me out of having to mince, but it keeps my hands from smelling like garlic. I always use it, especially when I'm making a recipe that calls for finely minced garlic, or minced fresh ginger, even.

BOX GRATER

I'm so old-fashioned when it comes to my box grater. I use it for everything. Whether it's for grating zucchini, carrots, cheese, or even to finely grate onions, it's a tool I use almost daily. I've already had to replace several box graters because I dull them out. Bonus: Using this tool helps you work on toning your upper arms.

CHEF'S KNIFE

If your budget allows you to have only one knife—and one knife only—let it be a chef's knife. Paring, bread, and Santoku knives are important and useful, but a chef's knife can be used for almost any task. When shopping, look for an 8-inch chef's knife made of stain-resistant carbon steel. As for a brand, we all would love to own a block of Shun knives, of course, but my last two sets have been Henckels and I absolutely adore them. They're affordable, the grips fit my hands perfectly, and they sharpen like a dream.

KITCHEN SCALE

The scale has proven to be another one of my useful kitchen gadgets. I use it for weighing dry ingredients for baked goods, as well as meat, cheeses, nuts—and pretty much anything else. I also find it handy for when I buy items like meat in bulk and want to break it down and package it by weight to store in the freezer.

CUTTING BOARDS

This may seem like a pretty obvious one, but I had to put cutting boards on the list. I love wood boards because they can easily convert into a nifty appetizer tray or bread and cheese server, which is particularly handy when you're entertaining. Maintenance is also easy enough: just rub food-grade mineral oil on them every six weeks. These inexpensive products are easy to find in most stores or online.

I use wood boards for everything except raw meat. For meat, I use a large plastic cutting board. It immediately goes in the dishwasher to sterilize after each use.

MESH STRAINERS OR SIFTERS

I have a set of nesting mesh strainers that I use for just about everything, since they are another multipurpose kitchen tool. You can use these for rinsing berries, herbs, lentils, and rice. I even strain the pulp out of my daughter's lemonade with one of these. Mesh strainers are also great for sifting dry ingredients when baking. Love them.

I sort of have a problem hoarding measuring devices (which is completely separate from my other obsession: hoarding serving bowls, foodie magazines, and vinegars!). In my opinion, you can't have too many measuring spoons or cups. There are so many times when I'm in the middle of cooking and I need to pause to rinse out a measuring cup that's already been used for another ingredient. It's just nice to have spares! I also don't like to take a teaspoon that has leftover vanilla extract in it (even after I give it a quick rinse) and stick it in the jar of cinnamon. As long as you have the space, you can never have *too* many measuring cups, spoons, or bowls.

Two sets of measuring cups and spoons will do the trick. (I have four sets of both measuring cups and spoons, which may be overdoing it a tad but has come in handy a time or two.) One set of measuring bowls or extra-large measuring cups is great for measuring large quantities of liquids, too, such as water for Homemade Broths (page 44). These are also great for mixing pancake or brownie batter.

FOOD PROCESSOR (REGULAR AND MINI)

I both hate and love my big, hunky, clunky, loud food processor. It's getting up there in years, and I may have to hold down the food chute for it to even work. If it wasn't for the fact that it makes preparing All-Purpose or Herbed Pie Crust (pages 49 and 50) a cinch, or pureeing large batches of salsa a dream, then I would forgo it and stick with my mini food processor.

My mini food processor is perfect for whipping up small batches of salad dressings, making Homemade Mayonnaise (page 25), chopping and blending herbs—there are millions of uses. I even use it to freshly grate Parmesan cheese for Spaghetti & Meatballs (page 235), and it makes my 5-Minute Avocado Spread (page 80) as easy as can be. If you can't tell, I love it to pieces. It's a total *must-have* in the kitchen.

BLENDER

Since the demise of my thirteen-year-old Oster, I have purchased a high-powered Vitamix blender. It has made my smoothies ultra-smooth and soups more velvety than ever.

If a Vitamix isn't in your budget, though, there are a ton of other brands that will do the job of pureeing, liquefying, and smoothing just fine. Be sure to buy a larger blender if you have the space so you can blend larger batches of soups, smoothies, and ingredients at once.

If you lack the space to house a blender, then an immersion blender is a great alternative for pureeing soups, applesauce, and even pesto!

STAND MIXER

While hand mixers are great for making Whipped Cream, Three Ways (page 293), I absolutely *love* my stand mixer. Not only does it handle my toughest cookie recipe like a champ, but it also shreds chicken and creams mashed potatoes like a dream. I can't imagine my life (or my kitchen) without this in it.

RICE COOKER

It's well documented on my website that I cannot make rice. I've tried it several times and it's either overcooked or way undercooked. The only way I can honestly say I make rice perfectly every time is with a rice cooker. Plus, it frees up the stovetop and will also keep the rice warm until the rest of the meal is ready to serve. Most rice cookers also have instructions on how to cook other grains like farro or quinoa. If you have the space, I highly recommend this life-saving appliance.

SKILLETS & SAUCEPANS

Obviously, you need pans to cook. I use mine pretty much every single day. My go-to pans are my set of All-Clad stainless steel that Pat bought me for our anniversary. I also rely on a set of Lodge cast-iron skillets in three different sizes. I love my small stainless 8-inch skillet for things like toasting nuts and spices, and my big 12-inch cast-iron skillet for searing off big hunks of meat.

DUTCH OVEN

I would like to thank Martha Stewart for turning me on to my first Dutch oven. I'm not exactly sure when it happened, but one day I was watching her intently wielding a large wooden spoon, sautéing onions with butter in her heavy, muted gray Dutch oven, and I knew at that moment that I needed to have one. I hit the lottery when I found a huge 5-quart red enameled cast-iron Dutch oven on clearance at Target. It isn't muted gray, but I love it all the same. Dutch ovens are great to use for big batches of chili, soup, or Beer-Braised Lamb Shanks (page 229).

ALUMINUM BAKING SHEETS

Whether it's baking cookies, roasting vegetables, or making garlic bread, a cook needs a set of sturdy metal baking sheets.

Tips for Easy, From-Scratch Cooking

Here's some advice for getting delicious from-scratch meals on the table quickly, and with your sanity intact!

REMEMBER YOUR *MISE EN PLACE*: This is just fancy talk for getting your ingredients prepped, measured, and organized before you even start cooking. It is a great time-saving practice: cooking will be less frustrating, and your cleanup will go by more quickly, too. Prep, prep, and do more prep so cooking can be a breeze.

CHECK EXPIRATION DATES: Checking the expiration or "use by" date on all ingredients is extremely important, but especially when it comes to baking. Expired baking powder and soda are the usual culprits for baked goods that turn out flat. These two ingredients do have a long shelf life, but if you don't bake a lot, the expiration date usually comes and goes before you realize it. Always keep an extra watchful eye on the expiration dates for yeast, baking soda, and baking powder.

ORGANIZE YOUR KITCHEN! I cannot express enough how it is extremely important to keep your cupboards, drawers, and pantry organized. While this is coming from the girl who never kept her room cleaned as a kid, a messy and disorganized kitchen is potentially dangerous, and keeping it clean should be taken seriously. Bonus: An organized kitchen will save you time as you cook and shop! Truly. You'll always know where to reach to find any ingredient, so you'll be able to quickly assess your fridge and pantry before each trip to the grocery store. Shopping lists will be a cinch. If your kitchen is organized, you'll never buy the same thing twice (and then have to find space for multiple packages again). Trust me on this; I was always notorious for buying an extra container of oatmeal or mayonnaise, because I couldn't see them hiding behind the mess in my pantry or fridge. You'll also save money if your kitchen is organized, simply because you'll never buy an ingredient you already have on hand.

PLAN YOUR MEALS IN ADVANCE: Another rule of thumb I follow is that I usually plan out a week of meals in advance. On a Sunday night, I will curl up with a pen and paper to draft a week's worth of meals. Once I have an idea of what I want to cook, I'll compile a list of all the ingredients I'll need. Next, I mosey on into my kitchen to catalog the ingredients I already have and what I might need to purchase on my next trip to the grocery store. Anything I need to buy is added to my list. This practice also helps me keep my pantry from getting low on any staple ingredient. By regularly and systematically checking in my pantry and fridge each week, I rarely, if ever, run out of a staple ingredient.

Simple Techniques

There are complicated recipes with a mile-long ingredients list, and then there are those recipes that aren't really a recipe at all. For example, hard-boiling eggs is simple enough, but some of us may need to google it just to remember how long they take to cook, right? (I've been there.)

Some of the "recipes" below are basics for everyday cooking; others are simple techniques that will take your from-scratch kitchen to new heights. You'll use them again and again in the recipes in this book, and they are fundamental for creating delicious from-scratch meals.

HARD-BOILED EGGS

I cannot tell you how many times I've hard-boiled eggs. All those Easters, all those salads . . . all those *eggs*! Every time I make them, I keep waiting to see the telltale olive green sign of an overcooked egg, and it just never happens. I'm sure there are a bunch of foolproof methods, but this is how I do it, and it works every time.

Place an even layer of eggs on the bottom of a pot. (Do not stack them or else they will end up cracking.) Fill the pot with cold water so it covers the eggs by an inch. Cover with a tight-fitting lid and bring to a boil. Once the water is at a full boil, turn off the heat and set a timer for 12 minutes. Meanwhile, fill a bowl with ice and cold water. When the time is up, use tongs to remove the eggs and immediately submerge them in the ice bath to stop the cooking. Peel them and they are good to go!

BALSAMIC REDUCTION

I discovered reducing balsamic way too late in life. Then one time I mixed reduced balsamic with honey and drizzled it all over prosciutto-wrapped, Gorgonzola-stuffed dates. And then I ate the whole plate. The end.

Pour the desired amount of balsamic vinegar into a saucepan and grab a whisk. Bring the balsamic to a simmer over medium heat. Simmer until it has reduced by half. It will thicken as it cools and should have the consistency of molasses.

CORNSTARCH SLURRY (AKA THE *BEST* WAY TO THICKEN A SAUCE)

Sometimes a sauce can be too thin, and no amount of reducing will help it thicken. We've all been there. The best way to rectify this situation is by making a quick cornstarch slurry.

Combine 1 tablespoon cornstarch with 1 tablespoon cold water for every cup of liquid in the pan. (I just eyeball it.) Bring the sauce to a bubble, stir in the slurry, and cook for 2 to 3 minutes.

CHARRED PEPPERS

Charring peppers is a great method to inject a little smoky flavor into a recipe. Charred peppers make for great garnishes, too. It's also the easiest way to remove the skin from a pepper. I love to char jalapeños, red bell peppers, and poblanos.

- GRILL METHOD: This is my go-to way to char. I don't have a gas stovetop, so when there isn't eighteen inches of snow on the ground, this is the route

I take. Heat your grill to medium-high. Place a pepper (or peppers) on the grates, close the lid, and let it char for 5 minutes. Rotate and repeat this process until all sides are charred. After 12 to 15 minutes, the skin should be black and blistered.

- GAS STOVETOP METHOD: Owning a gas stove makes this process even easier. Using metal tongs, hold the pepper over a medium-high to high flame, rotating it to create an even char.
- OVEN METHOD: This method is my alternative way to char peppers during the cooler months. First, preheat the broiler to high and crack the oven door. Place a washed pepper on a foil-lined, rimmed baking sheet and slide it under the broiler, rotating it every few minutes until it is charred.

Once you've charred your peppers using one of the methods above, pop them into a bowl, cover tightly with plastic wrap, and allow the steam to work its magic under the skins for 10 to 15 minutes. Peel and discard the skins, and the peppers are ready to be added to your favorite recipe or used as a garnish.

ROASTING VEGETABLES

Once I discovered the proper method of roasting vegetables, I proceeded to roast every vegetable in sight, and the result is always the same: perfection! Here are some key foolproof tips to perfectly roast your vegetables:

- Cut vegetables in uniform size so they cook evenly. Firmer and denser vegetables, like root vegetables, should be cut into smaller pieces. Tender vegetables (mushrooms, broccoli, etc.) should be cut into larger pieces, since they cook quickly and you don't want to overcook them.
- If you're roasting a few different vegetables together, place the firmer vegetables on one baking sheet and the more tender vegetable on a separate baking sheet. The tender veggie pan can be removed before the other pan is done to avoid overcooking.
- Roast veggies in a large, rimmed, metal baking sheet, *not* a glass baking dish

or a metal baking dish with tall sides, i.e., a brownie pan. The sides should be no higher than one inch; otherwise, you won't get the browned and crispy edges you're looking for. Metal is a conductor, so it will distribute the heat evenly to the vegetables; glass pans will cook your vegetables more slowly and prevent browning.

- Don't crowd the pan. It's always better to divide batches among a few baking sheets than it is to crowd them. The vegetables will just end up steaming themselves if they're piled on top of one another, resulting in a mushy, unevenly cooked batch.
- Season generously! Don't be shy with the oil—make sure to coat all the vegetables, even in those nooks and crannies. They should glisten. Also season with a few pinches of salt. I sprinkle vegetables with black pepper after roasting.
- Roast in a preheated 450 to 500°F oven. A hot oven will mean less time needed to roast, and the vegetables will brown better. Depending on the size and density of the vegetables you're cooking, you'll need to adjust cooking time by eye and touch. But for roasted broccoli, for example, which is something I make *a lot*, it's 12 to 15 minutes. Butternut squash or potatoes, if cut into smaller pieces, will take 20 to 30 minutes.

DIY BUTTERMILK

I use this quick trick when I don't have store-bought buttermilk at home. It's an excellent substitute for the real thing when I'm baking. I don't use it when I want to marinate chicken or if I'm making a Buttermilk Ranch Dressing & Dip (page 76)—that is when I make sure to have the real stuff on hand because texture is so important. But for baking, it works great. Here's what to do:

For every 1 cup of milk add 1 tablespoon of (strained) lemon juice or white vinegar. Let it stand for 5 to 8 minutes. It will thicken and curdle. Use it (even the curdled bits) in the recipe in place of buttermilk.

I toast nuts 99.9 percent of the time before using them in a recipe. Toasting brings out the natural oils and gives them a good color. And, of course, there is the delicious toasty flavor. Here's how to toast nuts:

In a small, dry skillet, scatter nuts in an even layer. Cook slowly over medium to medium-low heat until fragrant and slightly golden in color, 5 to 8 minutes. Be sure to watch carefully so they do not burn. All stovetops and ovens are not equal, so times may vary.

HAZELNUTS: The only nut I won't toast as I describe above is hazelnuts. Instead, stick those on a rimmed baking sheet and slide into a 350°F oven for 10 to 12 minutes. Next, pop them into a clean kitchen towel and shake them so the skins rub off.

ROASTING GARLIC

I love roasting garlic, mixing it with softened butter, and smearing it on bread—it's so unbelievably delicious. I also love it in Roasted Garlic Whipped Cauliflower (page 166). As an added bonus, the smell as you are roasting it is heavenly.

WHOLE GARLIC ROASTING: Peel the outer skins, leaving one thin layer covering the garlic bulb. Cut off the top third (or enough to expose every clove of garlic inside). Drizzle the bulb with a tablespoon of olive oil and wrap it tightly in foil. If you are roasting multiple heads of garlic, nestle them in a small baking dish and tightly cover the dish with foil. Bake in a preheated 375°F oven for 45 minutes. Allow to cool until they are safe to handle, and then squeeze out the luscious, golden cloves.

Try substituting honey for the oil to make honey roasted garlic. It is to die for!

INDIVIDUAL CLOVE ROASTING: Say you have a hankering to make roasted garlic butter, but you only need four cloves of roasted garlic. You could roast an entire head and just save the unused garlic in the fridge for another recipe. Or, you could roast individual cloves.

Place the desired number of garlic cloves on a sheet of heavy-duty aluminum foil. Drizzle them with a little olive oil, wrap tightly in the foil to create a pouch, and roast in a preheated 400°F oven for 20 to 25 minutes. Let cool until safe to handle and then peel the outer skin off each clove.

Essentially, browning butter is the process of slowly cooking out the water in butter and cooking the milk solids until they turn a toasty golden brown. It's a great way to ramp up flavor in a recipe, whether you're making something sweet or savory. I love mixing brown butter with maple syrup and pouring it over pancakes or French toast or tossing in a little lemon juice and spooning it over grilled tilapia. There are literally hundreds of ways in which to use brown butter. Here's how to make it:

Start by selecting a skillet to accommodate the amount of butter you'll be browning. For 8 tablespoons (1 stick) butter, I use a 10-inch skillet. I also use a stainless-steel skillet as opposed to a cast-iron skillet so I can see the milk solids brown and not risk burning them.

Cut the butter into tablespoons and drop them into the skillet. Melt the butter over medium heat, stirring continuously with a spatula so it will melt and cook evenly. The melted butter will begin to bubble and foam. This is the water evaporating out of the butter. Keep stirring.

Once the water has evaporated, the milk solids in the butter will start to turn a golden brown and smell amazingly nutty. It can go from golden to burned in seconds, so once the butter has browned, immediately remove it from the heat and pour it into a heat-safe dish.

COOKING WITH DRIED BEANS

While most will agree that cooking with soaked dried beans is best—especially when you're cooking from scratch—I do still use canned beans from time to time, usually when I don't plan well enough in advance. If I'm making a spur-of-the-moment chili, or decide at the last minute to add beans to a soup, I cheat. But if you have the time, and you've planned for a specific meal, soaking beans is completely easy and worth doing. They are delicious!

I typically measure ½ cup dried beans for every 1 cup cooked beans called for in a recipe. The dried beans will swell and nearly double in size during soaking, so this rule of thumb is best to follow.

OVERNIGHT SOAK METHOD

Sort the beans, discarding any suspicious beans or small pebbles that can sometimes be missed at the packaging facilities. Place the sorted beans in a mesh strainer and rinse them under cool water.

Place the rinsed beans in a large bowl and add water to cover by at least 2 inches. Allow the beans to soak overnight, or for 6 to 8 hours. Drain and rinse the beans.

To cook: Place the beans in a large pot and add hot water to cover. Tilt the lid a bit so the steam can escape and bring the water to a boil. Reduce the heat to maintain a simmer and cook gently until the beans are tender. The time varies based on the kind of beans you are using and how fresh they are, but this will generally take between 1 and 3 hours.

QUICK SOAK METHOD

Sort the beans, discarding any suspicious beans or small pebbles that can sometimes be missed at the packaging facilities. Place your sorted beans in a mesh strainer and rinse under cool water.

Place the rinsed beans in a pot and add hot water to cover by 2 inches. Bring to a rapid boil and cook for 2 minutes. Remove from the heat, cover, and let stand for 1 hour.

TO COOK: Place the beans in a large pot and add hot water to cover. Tilt the lid a bit so steam can escape and bring to a boil. Reduce the heat to maintain a simmer and cook gently until the beans are tender. The time varies based on the kind of beans being used and how fresh they are, but this will generally take between 1 and 3 hours.

It's always best to taste test a few beans from time to time as they cook to determine how much longer they will need and adjust the time accordingly.

If you want to use canned beans instead of soaking and cooking dried beans for any recipe in this book that calls for beans, I give you permission to *absolutely* go for it! Hey, I agree: canned beans are a time saver. Just drain and rinse the beans properly and you're good to go. No one will judge. Promise.

CHAPTER TWO

The Basics, from Scratch

It wasn't until I dove headfirst into from-scratch cooking that I really understood how easily I could elevate the food I cooked by making my own kitchen basics. When I say basics, I mean things like ketchup, mayonnaise, herb pestos, and seasoning blends—I could go on, but I'll keep the list short. It has been years since I've opened a can of cream-of-whatever soup or a preblended spice packet. Homemade *anything* is a thousand times better (and cheaper). And please don't get me started on homemade broths and salad dressings. Life changing.

Knowing what is going into the food I feed my family gives me insurmountable peace of mind. More important, it gives me bragging rights. Who doesn't love that? If bragging rights aren't what you're looking for, though, you'll definitely still be high-fiving yourself after a meal that you can proudly say is 100 percent from scratch. Going the extra mile to make these basic staples may take a smidgen extra time, but as you'll soon find out, it's well worth it. If you can set aside some time during one morning or afternoon to make a batch of homemade Chicken Broth or Vegetable Broth (pages 45, 46) to put in the freezer, for example, you'll have it on hand when you need it. (I like to measure out homemade broth in ice cube trays in the freezer so I can use smaller amounts in sauces and pasta dishes, too.)

In this chapter, you'll find many of my favorite and most frequently used basics, all of which can be used in other recipes throughout this entire book. I'm a believer in having options: sometimes you don't plan to make homemade ketchup a day in advance so you can whip up a batch of from-scratch barbecue sauce. Hey, I get it. But if you're new to the cooking-from-scratch world, half the fun is to try making even the simplest kitchen staple that you never thought to try at home. Ketchup is one of the most heavily used condiments in the world, and yet how many of us have ever actually made it?

With the recipes that follow, you can consider yourself well equipped with a collection of trusty, tried-and-true pantry and fridge basics that will help you get the whole from-scratch ball rolling.

Condiments & Staple Pantry Items

Homemade Mayonnaise

I'm a bit of a mayo snob. There, I said it. The texture of store-bought mayo has always made me cringe inwardly (and maybe outwardly, too). I've always found it overly thick and goopy, so I'd spread a microthin layer on my sandwich or bun so I wouldn't end up with a large glob in any one bite. This mayonnaise recipe makes mayo with a light texture, which I have zero problems spreading generously on my sandwiches. I've incorporated it into salad dressings, all kinds of aiolis, dips, and *anywhere* else mayonnaise is called for in a recipe. Not only is the texture more to my liking, it tastes better and is much healthier to boot.

I love using my mini food processor to make mayo. It frees up one hand so I can pour the oil at the same time. With this method, I can turn out a jar of homemade mayo in minutes. But feel free to go the "by hand" route. It will be amazing either way.

NOTE: Unlike its store-bought counterpart, homemade mayo lasts only a few days in the fridge. Luckily, it's a cinch to whip up, and is infinitely cheaper.

MAKES 1¼ CUPS • TOTAL TIME: 5 MINUTES

DIRECTIONS

- In the bowl of your mini food processor or blender, combine the egg, egg yolk, mustard, lemon juice, salt, and pepper (if using). Pulse to blend.

- With the processor running, slowly pour in the grape-seed oil through the feed tube (or the small holes in the lid) in a thin and steady stream. Taste and season with more salt and pepper as desired.

- Homemade mayonnaise will keep in an airtight container in the refrigerator for up to 3 days.

INGREDIENTS

1 large egg

1 large egg yolk

1 teaspoon Dijon mustard

1 tablespoon fresh lemon juice

½ teaspoon kosher salt, plus more as needed

¼ teaspoon freshly ground black pepper (optional)

1 cup grape-seed oil

Aiolis

Aioli is a fancy term people like to throw around in lieu of saying flavored mayonnaise. Making an aioli can elevate a plain sandwich or burger. It's a spectacular dip for french fries. You can pretty much throw whatever your heart desires into mayonnaise and poof! Insta-aioli. Here are a few of my personal favorites, each of which makes about 1 cup.

Lemon-Garlic Aioli

DIRECTIONS:

- In the bowl of a mini food processor, pulse the garlic until finely chopped. Add the mayonnaise, lemon zest, and lemon juice and pulse until smooth. Keep refrigerated until ready to use. Aioli should last, depending on how fresh the homemade mayonnaise is, for 2 to 3 days.

INGREDIENTS:

2 small cloves garlic

1 cup Homemade Mayonnaise (page 25)

½ teaspoon grated lemon zest

2 teaspoons fresh lemon juice

Chipotle-Lime Aioli

DIRECTIONS:

- In the bowl of a mini food processor, pulse the garlic, chipotle peppers, and adobo sauce until finely chopped. Add the mayonnaise, lime zest, and lime juice and pulse until smooth. Keep refrigerated until ready to use. Aioli should last, depending on how fresh the homemade mayonnaise is, for 2 to 3 days.

INGREDIENTS:

1 small clove garlic

2 small chipotle peppers in adobo

½ teaspoon adobo sauce

1 cup Homemade Mayonnaise (page 25)

¾ teaspoon grated lime zest

1 teaspoon fresh lime juice

Fresh Herb Aioli

INGREDIENTS:

1 small clove garlic

1 recipe Homemade Mayonnaise (page 25)

2 tablespoons chopped fresh chives

2 tablespoons chopped fresh flat-leaf parsley

1 teaspoon fresh lemon juice

DIRECTIONS:

• In the bowl of a mini food processor, pulse the garlic until finely chopped. Add the mayonnaise, chives, parsley, and lemon juice and pulse until smooth. Keep refrigerated until ready to use. Aioli should last, depending on how fresh the homemade mayonnaise is, for 2 to 3 days.

Ketchup

I truly believe people fall into one of two categories: those who consider ketchup a valid ingredient to use in cooking, and those who absolutely do not. Truthfully, I think I fall into both. Is that diplomatic or what? While I do love to make my own ketchup, and feel strongly that homemade ketchup trumps any brand on any grocery store shelf, I'll be honest and say that I don't always have the time to make it on a whim. If I'm making meat loaf and need a quarter cup ASAP, and I don't have any homemade ketchup on hand, I will just use store-bought. So I confess: I do keep a bottle of organic ketchup in the fridge at all times, but I only use it for what I call "culinary emergencies"—promise.

And I should probably also confess that I've yet to make my own tomato paste. It's on the list, but until then . . .

MAKES 2 CUPS • TOTAL TIME: 15 MINUTES TO OVERNIGHT

DIRECTIONS:

- In a medium bowl, combine the tomato paste, sugar, mustard, salt, allspice, cayenne, cloves, and turmeric. Pour in the vinegar, Worcestershire, and 2/3 cup water and stir until the sugar has dissolved and the mixture is smooth.

- Transfer to an airtight container and refrigerate for at least 3 hours or up to overnight so the flavors have a chance to develop.

- The ketchup will keep in an airtight container in the refrigerator for up to 3 weeks.

INGREDIENTS:

2 (6-ounce) cans tomato paste

2 tablespoons dark brown sugar

½ teaspoon ground mustard

½ teaspoon kosher salt

⅛ teaspoon ground allspice

⅛ teaspoon cayenne pepper

⅛ teaspoon ground cloves

⅛ teaspoon ground turmeric

¼ cup apple cider vinegar

1 teaspoon low-sodium Worcestershire sauce

SIMPLY SCRATCH TIP

It's easy to have fun with this ketchup recipe by adding fresh basil leaves or curry. You can up the turmeric for a fun twist, too—there are so many possibilities to make this traditional ketchup more exciting.

Sweet Barbecue Sauce

Who doesn't love a simple yet tasty barbecue sauce that requires zero chopping or simmering? I know I do! I set out to create my own barbecue sauce recipe after scanning the label on one of my favorite store-bought brands. Of course, I found a huge list of not-so-great ingredients on the label, so I was inspired to make my own, minus all the additives. We *love* this barbecue sauce for grilled chicken, among many other things. It's great as a sauce for grilling; it can be drizzled on a barbecue chicken pizza; it's a fantastic glaze for Cornbread & Leek Stuffed Pork Chops (page 228). Did I mention we like to lick it off the spoon as well? Because we *so* do. This is your basic barbecue sauce, and it's killer.

MAKES 3 CUPS • TOTAL TIME: 10 MINUTES (PLUS 2 TO 3 HOURS CHILLING)

DIRECTIONS:

- In a large bowl, combine the sugar, mustard, paprika, salt, and pepper. Add the ketchup, vinegar, and Worcestershire and whisk until the sugar has dissolved.

- Refrigerate until ready to use. This barbecue sauce will keep nicely in an airtight container in the refrigerator for 2 to 3 weeks.

INGREDIENTS:

1½ cups packed dark brown sugar

2½ teaspoons dry mustard

2 teaspoons paprika

1½ teaspoons kosher salt, or more to taste

¾ teaspoon coarsely ground black pepper

1¼ cups Ketchup (page 29)

½ cup red wine vinegar

1 tablespoon Worcestershire sauce

SIMPLY SCRATCH TIP

This sauce is best after a few hours in the fridge, which helps to round out the flavors. For a spicy and smoky sauce, consider adding a minced chipotle pepper and a little of the adobo for a delicious kick.

Pestos

There are numerous ways to make pesto interesting: instead of using the traditional basil recipe, you can switch up the herbs or add different kinds of nuts or cheese. Pesto is a frequently made condiment in our house, and for me, the sky is the limit with this basic staple.

I use it as a sauce instead of a traditional red sauce on our pizzas. I'll toss it with pasta, or put it into a grilled cheese sandwich along with fresh slices of tomato and mozzarella cheese. I'll even turn pesto into a vinaigrette to use in my Roasted Beets with Parsley Pesto Vinaigrette (page 169).

A good pesto is true perfection and can be used for many different things.

Basil Pesto

DIRECTIONS:

- In a small, dry skillet, toast the pine nuts over medium-low heat for 3 to 5 minutes, until lightly golden in color and fragrant. Keep a close eye on them so they do not burn. Transfer to a clean dish to cool.

- Meanwhile, bring a large pot of water to a boil and fill a large bowl with ice and cold water. Drop the basil leaves into the boiling water and blanch for 10 to 15 seconds, stirring occasionally. Use tongs to immediately remove the basil and plunge it into the ice bath. Drain and pat dry.

- Transfer the basil to a food processor and add the toasted pine nuts, Parmesan, garlic, lemon zest and juice, salt, and pepper.

- With the food processor running, slowly drizzle in the olive oil. Blend until smooth. If stored in an airtight container with a layer of olive oil over top (adding more after each use) in the refrigerator, it will keep for 2 to 3 months.

INGREDIENTS:

⅓ cup pine nuts

2 cups packed fresh basil leaves

½ cup finely grated Parmesan cheese

2 cloves garlic, coarsely chopped

Zest and juice of 1 lemon

½ teaspoon kosher salt

⅛ teaspoon coarsely ground black pepper

1 cup extra-virgin olive oil

Cilantro Pesto

INGREDIENTS:

Heaping ½ cup slivered blanched almonds

1 large clove garlic, smashed

Leaves from 2 large bunches fresh cilantro

3 tablespoons Cotija cheese

1 teaspoon kosher salt

Juice of 1 medium lime

½ cup olive oil

DIRECTIONS:

- In a small, dry skillet, toast the almonds over medium-low heat for 3 to 5 minutes, or until golden and fragrant. Transfer to a clean dish to cool.

- In the bowl of a food processor, combine the garlic and toasted almonds and pulse until coarsely chopped.

- Add the cilantro, cheese, salt, and lime juice. Pulse a few times until coarsely ground. With the food processor running, slowly drizzle in the olive oil. Blend until smooth. If stored in an airtight container with a layer of olive oil on top (adding more after each use) in the refrigerator, it will keep for 2 to 3 months.

Parsley Pesto

INGREDIENTS:

DIRECTIONS:

- In a small, dry skillet, toast the walnuts over medium-low heat for 3 to 5 minutes, or until fragrant. Keep a close eye on them so they do not burn. Transfer to a clean dish to cool.

- In the bowl of a food processor, combine the garlic, toasted walnuts, parsley, scallions, Parmesan, salt, red pepper flakes, and black pepper and pulse until coarsely chopped.

- With the food processor running, slowly drizzle in the olive oil in a thin, steady stream. Halfway through, stop and scrape down the sides of the bowl. Taste and season with more salt, if desired, and process until smooth. If stored in an airtight container with a thin layer of olive oil on top (adding more after each use) in the refrigerator, it will keep for 2 to 3 months.

1 cup walnuts

4 cloves garlic, coarsely chopped

Leaves from 1 large bunch fresh parsley, coarsely chopped

5 scallions, light green and dark green parts only, coarsely chopped

½ cup freshly grated Parmesan cheese

½ teaspoon kosher salt

¼ teaspoon red pepper flakes

Coarsely ground black pepper

½ cup olive oil

SIMPLY SCRATCH TIP

These pesto recipes can easily be doubled and then frozen for later.

To store in the fridge: Pour pesto into an airtight container before covering with a thin layer of olive oil. The oil will help insulate the pesto, preventing oxidation and keeping it fresh for a longer period of time, 2 to 3 months and possibly longer.

To freeze: Spoon about 2 tablespoons of pesto into each slot in an ice cube tray. Cover with a thin layer of olive oil and freeze for 2 to 3 hours or overnight. Pop the pesto cubes out of the tray and place into a freezer-safe resealable bag. Store the pesto cubes for up to 3 months in the freezer.

Seasoning Blends

I've created six seasoning blends that I use all the time. With these mixes on hand, your kitchen will be well stocked to add a flavor boost to meals morning, noon, and night!

I use the All-Purpose Seasoned Salt (page 38) to season my morning fried eggs, or when making my family's favorite fried egg side dish, Breakfast Home Fries (page 104). The adobo seasoning works well with pretty much anything on and off the grill, and it's especially handy when making my Spicy Southwest Dip (page 70). The Italian seasoning will blow your mind (in a good way!). Try sprinkling it on tomatoes with a little salt and pepper before roasting them. Unbelievable. Promise.

Making your own seasoning blends takes just a few minutes and is a great way to use up those spices in your cupboard before they expire. I love to make my own spice mixes to save money. Who doesn't love that?

NOTE: I always rub dried oregano (and sometimes dried basil) in the palm of my hand before adding to sauces, dressings, and seasoning blends. By crushing the leaves they become smaller, and I feel it releases more of the herbs' flavors. And plus, I've always seen my mom do it this way.

Adobo Seasoning

1 tablespoon onion powder

1 tablespoon garlic powder

1 teaspoon freshly ground black pepper

1 teaspoon dried oregano, crushed in your palm

½ teaspoon ground turmeric

MAKES ABOUT 3 TABLESPOONS • TOTAL TIME: 5 MINUTES

DIRECTIONS:

- Combine all the ingredients in an airtight container and store in a dry, dark place for up to 6 months.

All-Purpose Seasoned Salt

INGREDIENTS:

2 tablespoons fine sea salt

1 tablespoon paprika

¾ teaspoon sugar

¾ teaspoon ground turmeric

½ teaspoon garlic powder

¼ teaspoon onion powder

⅛ teaspoon cayenne pepper

MAKES 3 TABLESPOONS • TOTAL TIME: 5 MINUTES

DIRECTIONS:

- Combine all the ingredients in an airtight container and store in a dry, dark place for up to 6 months.

Poultry Seasoning

MAKES 3 TABLESPOONS • TOTAL TIME: 5 MINUTES

DIRECTIONS:

- In a spice grinder or using a mortar and pestle, combine 2 teaspoons of the thyme, the marjoram, and rosemary. Blend until finely ground. Transfer to an airtight container and add the remaining 1 teaspoon thyme, the nutmeg, paprika, and sage. Store in a dry, dark place for up to 6 months.

INGREDIENTS:

3 teaspoons dried thyme

1 ½ teaspoons dried marjoram

1 teaspoon dried rosemary

½ teaspoon freshly grated nutmeg

2 teaspoons paprika

2 teaspoons ground sage

Fajita Seasoning

MAKES 3 TABLESPOONS • TOTAL TIME: 5 MINUTES

DIRECTIONS:

- Combine all the ingredients in an airtight container and store in a dry, dark place for up to 6 months.

NOTE: You can use this seasoning blend in place of store-bought fajita seasoning packets. Sprinkle over the top of cooked chicken or beef in a skillet, pour in ¼ to ½ cup water, and bring to a simmer. Cook until reduced and thick.

INGREDIENTS:

1 tablespoon cornstarch

2 teaspoons chili powder

1 teaspoon kosher salt

1 teaspoon paprika

½ teaspoon sugar

½ teaspoon onion powder

½ teaspoon ground cumin

¼ teaspoon garlic powder

¼ teaspoon cayenne pepper

Italian Seasoning

INGREDIENTS:

1 tablespoon dried marjoram

1 tablespoon dried basil

1 tablespoon dried oregano, crushed in your palm

1 tablespoon dried parsley

1½ teaspoons ground sage

½ teaspoon dried thyme, crumbled in your palm

½ teaspoon dried rosemary, crumbled in your palm

MAKES ⅓ CUP • TOTAL TIME: 5 MINUTES

DIRECTIONS:

- Combine all the ingredients in an airtight container and store in a dry, dark place for up to 6 months.

Taco Seasoning

INGREDIENTS:

1 tablespoon ancho chili powder

1½ teaspoons ground cumin

1 teaspoon kosher salt

½ teaspoon coarsely ground black pepper

½ teaspoon paprika

¼ teaspoon dried oregano, ground in your palm

¼ teaspoon garlic powder

¼ teaspoon onion powder

⅛ teaspoon red pepper flakes, or more to taste

This recipe is equivalent to one packet of store-bought taco seasoning and can easily be doubled.

MAKES 2½ TABLESPOONS • TOTAL TIME: 5 MINUTES

DIRECTIONS:

- Combine all the ingredients in an airtight container and store in a dry, dark place for up to 6 months.

SIMPLY SCRATCH TIP

To make a sauce version for tacos or nachos, cook 1 pound ground beef. Drain off all but 2 tablespoons of the rendered fat from the pan. Sprinkle with the Taco Seasoning and 1 tablespoon all-purpose flour. Stir until the fat in the pan is absorbed and cook for 1 minute. Pour in ¼ cup water and stir until thickened. Use immediately.

Condensed Cream Soups

I remember the precise moment when I discovered I could make cream-of-*anything* soup. It was as if an imaginary lightbulb lit up above my head, like I had cracked some kind of code. I was attempting to make my family's beloved cheesy potatoes 100 percent from scratch for an Easter dinner. Typically, the recipe calls for a can of condensed creamed soup to round out the texture of the potatoes, but I was braving my first attempt at using a from-scratch equivalent. My family was going to be my taste testers, so there was a little (okay, a lot of) pressure not to disappoint them. I crossed my fingers after I slid the pan into the oven—praying that the dish would at least be edible, if not delicious—and when I finally snagged a bite, my eyes rolled back in my head. It was loads better than the recipe we'd come to love over the years. I realized I could now breathe new life into recipes that call for condensed soup by swapping out the canned soup for a little butter, flour, homemade broth, and a few fresh ingredients. Easy-peasy—and, you guys, seriously delicious.

These two condensed soup recipes are perfect substitutes for most recipes out there that call for a can of condensed soup, whether you're making casseroles, side dishes, or gravies served over chicken or beef. It's amazing what a few simple ingredients can do to ramp up the flavor. And I could literally eat a bowl of either condensed soup and not feel the least bit ashamed about it—perfect for a cold fall day.

NOTE: You can store either of these soups in an airtight container for 3 to 4 days in the fridge—or freeze and slowly defrost in a saucepan over low heat when needed. Use in any recipe that calls for canned condensed soup.

Also, if you are adding this to recipes that call for salt and pepper, season the dish you are making with a light hand.

Cream of Chicken Soup

INGREDIENTS:

3 tablespoons unsalted butter

1 small shallot, minced (about ¼ cup)

1 clove garlic, minced

2½ tablespoons unbleached all-purpose flour

½ cup Chicken Broth (page 45)

½ cup whole milk

Pinch of kosher salt

⅛ teaspoon coarsely ground black pepper

MAKES 1¼ CUPS (THE EQUIVALENT OF 1 "CAN" OF STORE-BOUGHT CONDENSED SOUP) • TOTAL TIME: 30 MINUTES

DIRECTIONS:

- In a 10-inch skillet, melt the butter over medium heat. Add the shallot and garlic, stir, and sauté for 5 minutes or until just starting to soften.

- Sprinkle in the flour, stir, and cook for 1 to 2 minutes. While whisking, pour in the chicken broth and milk and continue to whisk until smooth. Simmer until thick and season with the salt and pepper.

Cream of Mushroom Soup

MAKES 1¼ CUPS (THE EQUIVALENT OF 1 "CAN" OF STORE-BOUGHT CONDENSED SOUP) • TOTAL TIME: 30 MINUTES

INGREDIENTS:

3 tablespoons unsalted butter

1 small shallot, minced (about ¼ cup)

½ cup minced cremini mushrooms

2½ tablespoons unbleached all-purpose flour

½ cup Vegetable Broth (page 46)

½ cup whole milk

Pinch of kosher salt

⅛ teaspoon coarsely ground black pepper

DIRECTIONS:

- In a 10-inch skillet, melt the butter over medium heat. Add the shallot, stir, and sauté for 3 to 5 minutes, or until just soft. Add the mushrooms, stir, and cook for 2 to 3 minutes.

- Sprinkle in the flour and cook for a minute or two. While whisking, pour in the vegetable broth and whole milk and continue whisking until smooth.

- Simmer until thickened, 5 to 8 minutes, then season with salt and pepper.

Homemade Broths

Homemade broth is absolutely without a doubt the easiest thing to make. Basically, all you need to do is chop some vegetables, throw everything into a pot, cover with water, bring to a boil, and then simmer your broth on the back burner of your stove for an hour or two. I typically set aside a morning for making both chicken and vegetable broth, then I seal it all up in 2-cup reusable containers (the environment will thank you for this!). I just pop the containers into my freezer, and I'm done. Make these broths and you'll no doubt feel triumphant knowing you just stocked your kitchen with homemade goodness to use in soups, stews, and more. I make my broth without any added salt—this way, I'm in control of how much salt goes into a dish, since most store-bought brands of broth come salted. Besides being so incredibly simple, homemade broth is healthy, affordable, and most importantly more flavorful than store-bought. It's so very rewarding to make a big pot.

Chicken Broth

MAKES 10 TO 11 CUPS • TOTAL TIME: 3½ HOURS PLUS OVERNIGHT

DIRECTIONS:

- Place all the ingredients in a large stockpot. Pour in 12 cups water, cover, and bring to a boil over high heat. Once at a boil, reduce the heat to low and simmer for 3 hours. If any foam appears at the top, skim it off and discard.

- Use tongs to remove the chicken pieces and set aside. Line a fine-mesh sieve with cheesecloth and set it over a large bowl. Slowly pour the broth through the sieve to strain out the herbs and veggies. Discard the solids in the sieve. Debone and shred the chicken to use for another purpose, like my Southwest Chicken Chili (page 133).

- Let the broth cool, then cover and refrigerate overnight. Skim any congealed fat off the top before using or storing.

INGREDIENTS:

4 pounds skinless, bone-in chicken pieces

2 celery stalks, plus any leafy tops, coarsely chopped

2 carrots, unpeeled, coarsely chopped

1 yellow onion, unpeeled, cut into eighths

10 to 12 sprigs fresh parsley

1 bay leaf

2 sprigs fresh thyme

14 whole black peppercorns

Vegetable Broth

INGREDIENTS

4 ounces mushrooms, wiped clean with a damp cloth and left whole

3 celery stalks, plus any leafy tops, coarsely chopped

2 parsnips, unpeeled, coarsely chopped

2 carrots, unpeeled, coarsely chopped

1 yellow onion, unpeeled, cut into eighths

1 leek, white and light green parts only, coarsely chopped and soaked in cold water to remove any sand or grit

3 sprigs fresh thyme

1 bay leaf

10 to 12 sprigs fresh parsley

14 whole black peppercorns

MAKES 10 TO 11 CUPS • TOTAL TIME: 1 HOUR 15 MINUTES

DIRECTIONS:

- Place all the ingredients in a large stockpot. Pour in 12 cups water and bring to a boil over high heat. Once at a boil, reduce the heat to low, cover, and simmer for 1 hour.

- Line a fine-mesh sieve with cheesecloth and set it over a large bowl. Slowly pour the broth through the sieve to strain out the herbs and veggies. Discard the solids in the sieve.

- Let the broth cool before storing.

SIMPLY SCRATCH TIP

To defrost broth, heat on low in the microwave or run lukewarm water over the top of the container until thawed.

For smaller broth portions, spoon a few tablespoons of broth into ice cube trays and freeze. Remove and store in a freezer-safe container or resealable bag.

Baking, Bread & Starches

All-Purpose Pie Crust

One crust for all things pie-related. The end.

MAKES TWO 9-INCH PIE CRUSTS • TOTAL TIME: 50 MINUTES

DIRECTIONS:

- In the bowl of a food processor, combine the flour, salt, and butter and pulse until the pieces of butter are the size of peas and the mixture is crumbly; do not overmix.

- Add the ice water 1 tablespoon at a time, pulsing after each addition, until the dough comes together in large clumps and resembles coarse, wet sand. Divide the dough in half, form into round discs, and wrap in plastic wrap. Refrigerate for 30 minutes.

- On a lightly floured surface, roll out one disc of dough into an even 12-inch round and lay it over a 9-inch pie plate, leaving about 1 inch overhanging the edge. Fold the overhanging dough under to form a rim and crimp with your fingertips. Fill as desired.

- If your pie will have a top crust, roll out the second disc of dough. (If you're not using the second disc of dough, see the Simply Scratch Tip on page 50 for storing instructions.) Set the dough over the filling, fold the edge under the edge of the bottom crust, and crimp. Cut a few vents in the center of the dough to let the steam escape.

INGREDIENTS:

2¼ cups unbleached all-purpose flour

1 teaspoon kosher salt

1 cup (2 sticks) ice-cold unsalted butter, cut into pieces

6 to 8 tablespoons ice water

VARIATION: HERBED PIE CRUST: For savory dishes, follow instructions for making basic pie crust. Once the ingredients are combined, turn the dough crumbles out onto a clean surface, sprinkle with fresh herbs (2 tablespoons each minced parsley and snipped chives, and 2 teaspoons chopped thyme leaves) and quickly fold them into the crumbles. Divide the dough in half and place onto two separate pieces of plastic wrap. Gather the sides of the plastic wrap and shape into discs. Refrigerate for 30 minutes before rolling out.

SIMPLY SCRATCH TIP

Pie dough keeps very well in the freezer! Divide the dough in half, form into discs, and wrap each tightly in both plastic wrap and then heavy-duty aluminum foil before freezing. You'll need to thaw them before rolling, which could take an hour or two. Alternatively, roll out one disc of dough and fit it into your desired pie plate. Crimp the edges and carefully wrap the dough-lined pie plate in heavy-duty aluminum foil, then freeze. The second option allows you to have a ready-to-use pie crust that can go directly from freezer to oven. Just increase the baking time by a few minutes!

Pizza Dough

I've always said that the more you make bread dough, the easier it gets. So, whether it's dough for pizza or for homemade pita bread, the more you dip your toes in, so to speak, the more comfortable you'll feel with the process. I've used these doughs for both sweet and savory recipes like breadsticks, calzones, and pumpkin spice knots (a recipe you can find on my blog). This pizza dough is easy and extremely versatile.

Classic Pizza Dough

INGREDIENTS:

Heaping ½ teaspoon honey

1 cup warm water (110 to 115°F)

1 (¼-ounce) packet active dry yeast (2¼ teaspoons)

2 teaspoons olive oil

2½ cups unbleached all-purpose flour, plus more for dusting

¾ teaspoon kosher salt

MAKES ENOUGH DOUGH FOR 1 LARGE, 2 MEDIUM, OR 4 PERSONAL-SIZE PIZZAS • TOTAL TIME: 1 HOUR 25 MINUTES

DIRECTIONS:

- In the bowl of a stand mixer fitted with the paddle attachment, stir together the honey and warm water. Sprinkle in the yeast and let it sit and proof for 10 minutes.

- Pour in 1 teaspoon of the olive oil, the flour, and the salt. Mix on low until just combined. Switch over to the dough hook attachment. Continue mixing until the dough pulls easily from the sides of the bowl.

- Put the remaining 1 teaspoon olive oil in a large, clean bowl. Form the dough into a ball and place it in the oiled bowl, turning it to coat in oil. Use the dough to coat the sides of the bowl with oil as well.

- Cover the dough with a tea towel, place in a warm, dry spot, and let rise for 1 hour, or until doubled in size.

- Punch down the dough until it deflates and then reshape it into a ball. Lightly flour a work surface and the top of the dough. Using either your fingers or a lightly floured rolling pin, stretch or roll the dough out to fit your pan.

- Follow the cooking temperature and times indicated in your pizza recipe.

Whole Wheat Pizza Dough

MAKES ENOUGH DOUGH FOR 1 LARGE, 2 MEDIUM, OR 4
PERSONAL-SIZE PIZZAS • TOTAL TIME: 1 HOUR 25 MINUTES

INGREDIENTS:

Heaping ½ teaspoon honey

1 cup warm water (110 to 115°F)

1 (¼-ounce) packet active dry yeast (2¼ teaspoons)

2 teaspoons olive oil

1 cup whole wheat flour

1½ cups unbleached all-purpose flour

¾ teaspoon kosher salt

DIRECTIONS:

- In the bowl of a stand mixer fitted with the paddle attachment, stir together the honey and warm water. Sprinkle in the yeast and let it sit and proof for 10 minutes.

- Pour in 1 teaspoon of the olive oil, both flours, and the salt. Mix on low until just combined. Switch over to the dough hook attachment. Continue mixing until the dough pulls easily from the sides of the bowl.

- Put the remaining 1 teaspoon olive oil in a large, clean bowl. Form the dough into a ball and place it in the oiled bowl, turning it to coat in oil. Use the dough to coat the sides of the bowl with the oil as well.

- Cover the dough with a tea towel, place in a warm, dry spot, and let rise for 1 hour, or until doubled in size.

- Punch down the dough until it deflates and then reshape it into a ball. Lightly flour a work surface and the top of the dough. Using either your fingers or a lightly floured rolling pin, stretch or roll the dough out to fit your pan.

- Follow the cooking temperature and times indicated in your pizza recipe.

SIMPLY SCRATCH TIP

Both pizza dough recipes can be made up to 3 days in advance. Just keep the dough covered and refrigerated and let it come to room temperature 30 minutes to 1 hour before using.

Easy French Bread

INGREDIENTS:

1 cup warm water (110 to 115°F)

1 (¼-ounce) packet rapid-rise yeast (2¼ teaspoons)

2½ cups unbleached all-purpose flour

¾ teaspoon kosher salt

1 teaspoon olive oil

1 large egg (optional)

2 tablespoons water or milk (optional)

This recipe probably gets the most traffic in my house. I use it to make Italian-Seasoned (or plain) Bread Crumbs (page 58), Croutons (page 59), French bread pizzas, and garlic bread. It's ridiculously simple and pretty darn amazing.

MAKES 1 LOAF • TOTAL TIME: 1 HOUR 45 MINUTES

DIRECTIONS:

- Pour the warm water into the bowl of a stand mixer fitted with the paddle attachment. Sprinkle the rapid-rise yeast over the water and let it sit and proof for 10 minutes.

- With the mixer running, slowly add 1 cup of the flour and the salt and mix until just combined. Switch to the dough hook and gradually add the rest of the flour. Mix on low speed until the dough is smooth and tacky.

- Grease a large bowl with the olive oil. Form the dough into a ball and place it in the oiled bowl, turning it to coat in oil.

- Cover the dough with a damp tea towel and place the bowl in a warm, dry spot. Let it rise for 1 hour or until doubled in size.

- If desired, beat together the egg and water to make an egg wash. Set aside.

- Line a rimmed baking sheet with parchment paper or a silicone baking mat. Punch down the dough and form it into a long log shape. Place it on the lined baking sheet and brush with the egg wash (if using). Cut shallow slits on the top of the dough and then slide into a cold, un-preheated oven.

- Heat the oven to 375ºF (while the loaf is in the oven) and bake for 30 minutes.

- Let cool slightly before slicing and serving.

Rustic Pita Bread

Making homemade pita bread is easier than it sounds. All it takes is a simple bread dough, which you roll out thin and set on the wire racks of a very, *very* hot oven. As it bakes, it puffs up like a hot air balloon in the center, creating that pocket where you can stuff any number of delicious things. The key to soft, fluffy pita bread is first to try not to overbake the bread in the oven—4 to 5 minutes is all it should take; second, have a couple of rimmed baking sheets and two damp tea towels ready. The damp towels will help trap steam from the hot pitas to soften them so they will collapse and not remain puffed up.

As for what to stuff into them . . . try the Greek Lamb Pita Pockets on page 146.

MAKES 8 PITAS • TOTAL TIME: ABOUT 2 HOURS

DIRECTIONS:

- In the bowl of a mixer fitted with the dough hook, stir together the warm water and sugar until the sugar has dissolved. Stir in the yeast and let it sit and proof for 10 minutes.

- With the mixer on low, gradually add 1 tablespoon of the olive oil, the flour, and the salt. Mix until the flour is mostly incorporated, then increase the speed slightly and let the machine knead the dough for 3 to 4 minutes, or until soft and barely sticky.

- Put the remaining 1 teaspoon olive oil in a large, clean bowl. Form the dough into a ball and place it in the oiled bowl, turning it to coat in oil. Use the dough to coat the sides of the bowl in oil as well.

- Cover the dough with a tea towel, place it in a warm, dry spot, and let rise for 1 hour and 30 minutes, or until doubled in size.

INGREDIENTS:

1 cup plus 2 tablespoons warm water (110 to 115°F)

1½ teaspoons sugar

1½ teaspoons active dry yeast

1 tablespoon plus 1 teaspoon olive oil

3 cups unbleached all-purpose flour, plus more for dusting

1 teaspoon kosher salt

- Once the dough has risen, preheat the oven to 500°F and place the rack in the center.

- Punch down the dough and turn it out onto a lightly floured work surface. With floured hands, roll the dough into a 12-inch-long rope. Cut the dough into eight equal pieces. Roll the pieces into balls and cover with a damp tea towel. Working in batches of two, use a rolling pin to roll two dough balls at a time into rounds about 7 inches in diameter.

- Place two of the rounds at a time directly onto the oven rack, setting them an inch apart. Bake for 4 to 5 minutes, or until puffed in the center and lightly golden around the edges. Remove and place on a rimmed baking sheet or large platter and cover with a damp tea towel to soften and cool. Repeat with the remaining dough.

- Once cool, serve immediately or store in a plastic bag in the refrigerator for a couple of days.

Italian-Seasoned Bread Crumbs

INGREDIENTS:

8 ounces day-old Easy French Bread (page 54), cut into cubes (about 4 cups)

2 tablespoons Italian Seasoning (page 40)

½ teaspoon kosher salt

This is one of my favorite basics yet. It's easy and tastes infinitely better than store-bought versions. Try these Italian-seasoned bread crumbs in your next meat loaf and you will not be disappointed.

MAKES ABOUT 2 CUPS • TOTAL TIME: 30 MINUTES

DIRECTIONS:

- Preheat the oven to 325ºF.

- In the bowl of a food processor, pulse the bread cubes until finely ground crumbs have formed. Pour the crumbs into a medium bowl and add the Italian seasoning (or omit to make plain crumbs) and salt. Stir to combine. Spread the crumbs out in an even layer on a rimmed baking sheet and bake in 5-minute intervals for about 20 minutes, or until toasted and golden brown. Watch carefully so they do not burn.

- Let cool in the pan for 30 minutes before using or storing. Store in an airtight container at room temperature for up to 2 weeks.

Croutons

If I ever have extra bread lying around, I always, always use it for croutons. Making your own croutons really makes a world of difference. And it's easy. I mean, yes, it's essentially twice-baked bread, so of course it's simple! But the difference in taste (and texture) between buying croutons versus tossing cubed bread with a drizzle of olive oil, salt, and pepper and throwing it into the oven for 10 to 12 minutes—it's unreal. (Did I mention it's simple?!) The key? You need to use good-quality bread like sourdough, multigrain, or even my Easy French Bread recipe. The hard part? Trying to get the croutons to the table, since people are *always* stealing them off the pan! Myself included. Oops!

We love these croutons in a salad, with a bowl of soup, or as a snack. Seriously, croutons are a legitimate snack in our house. Try it.

MAKES 4 CUPS • TOTAL TIME: 20 TO 22 MINUTES

DIRECTIONS:

- Preheat the oven to 400°F.

- In a large bowl, toss the bread with the olive oil, salt, and pepper until generously coated.

- Divide the bread between two rimmed baking sheets and bake for 10 to 12 minutes, or until golden brown and toasted. Let the croutons cool before using. They will keep for 1 to 2 days in a resealable bag on the counter.

INGREDIENTS:

4 cups cubed sourdough or multigrain bread

3 tablespoons olive oil

¾ teaspoon kosher salt

¼ teaspoon freshly ground black pepper

SIMPLY SCRATCH TIP

Once you have these down, try changing things up by adding your favorite spices. I like using Italian Seasoning (page 40) or a sprinkle of Old Bay.

Honey Graham Crackers

1½ cups whole wheat flour

1½ cups unbleached all-purpose flour

1 teaspoon baking powder

¾ teaspoon salt

½ teaspoon baking soda

¾ teaspoon ground cinnamon

½ teaspoon freshly grated nutmeg

¼ teaspoon ground cardamom

8 tablespoons (1 stick) unsalted butter, at room temperature

⅓ cup packed dark brown sugar

⅓ cup honey

1½ teaspoons pure vanilla extract

½ cup heavy cream

These homemade graham crackers are not overly sweet and have just the right amount of spice from the cinnamon, nutmeg, and cardamom. My daughters love them. My favorite way to eat them is with a smear of peanut butter and a few chocolate chips on top. I also love to grind them into a crumb for the crust of my New York–Style Cheesecake (page 279).

One final note: To quote my kids, "These are better than store-bought."

Enough said.

MAKES ABOUT 50 (2½ BY 2½-INCH) CRACKERS • TOTAL TIME: 3 HOURS

DIRECTIONS:

- In a large bowl, sift together both flours, the baking powder, salt, baking soda, cinnamon, nutmeg, and cardamom. Set aside.

- In the bowl of a stand mixer fitted with the paddle attachment, cream together the butter, brown sugar, honey, and vanilla.

- Spoon in the flour mixture, alternating with the heavy cream, scraping down the sides of the bowl with a spatula as needed. Once the dough forms, it should be firm and resemble sugar cookie dough. Divide the dough in half, form into rectangular discs, wrap in plastic wrap, and refrigerate for 2 hours.

- Preheat the oven to 350°F. Line two baking sheets with silicone baking mats.

- On a lightly floured work surface, roll out one dough disc to ⅛ inch thick. Using a 2½ by 2½-inch square cutter (or measure with a ruler), cut squares from the dough and place them about ¼ of an inch apart on the baking sheets.

- Bake for 10 to 12 minutes, or until the edges are golden brown.

- Allow the graham crackers to cool on the pan for 5 minutes before transferring to a wire rack and repeat with the second disc of dough. Once cool, store in an airtight container at room temperature for 1 to 2 weeks.

SIMPLY SCRATCH TIP

For a little extra sweetness, sometimes I sprinkle a little turbinado sugar on top before baking.

Buttermilk Biscuits

2 cups unbleached all-purpose flour, plus more for dusting

1 tablespoon baking powder

¾ teaspoon kosher salt

¼ teaspoon baking soda

6 tablespoons (¾ stick) unsalted butter, cubed and chilled in the freezer

¾ cup plus 1 tablespoon cold buttermilk

I'm a Homemade Sausage Gravy over Buttermilk Biscuits (page 100) kind of girl, but my husband prefers to smother his biscuits with strawberry jam, and my girls just eat them plain. They're good no matter how you serve them.

There is one rule of thumb that guarantees you'll turn out tender, flaky biscuits every time: only use cold, cold, *COLD* butter and buttermilk—I keep them both chilled until the moment I'm ready to use them. This ensures the cold bits of butter will stay firm and won't melt before baking. Following this simple rule will cause the butter to basically explode when the biscuits hit the hot oven, and leaves pockets of air behind. That's how you get perfect, flaky, buttery biscuits.

MAKES 10 BISCUITS • TOTAL TIME: 35 MINUTES

DIRECTIONS:

- Preheat the oven to 425ºF and position the rack in the center. Line a baking sheet with a silicone baking mat or parchment paper.

- In a large bowl, whisk together the flour, baking powder, salt, and baking soda. Cut the butter into the flour mixture with a pastry blender until the mixture resembles coarse crumbs, about 5 minutes.

- Make a well in the center of the butter and flour mixture. Pour in ¾ cup of the buttermilk and stir until just combined.

- Turn the dough out onto a lightly floured work surface and form into a rectangle about ½ inch thick.

- Use a 3-inch round biscuit cutter to stamp out 8 biscuits, then gather up the scraps to make 2 more biscuits.

- Transfer the biscuits to the prepared baking sheet. Indent the top of each biscuit with your finger. Brush the tops of the biscuits with the remaining tablespoon of buttermilk.

- Bake until browned, 10 to 12 minutes.

Buttermilk Pancakes

I reserve pancake making for the weekends. My daughter Malloree's *favorite* breakfast of all breakfasts is a stack of heavily buttered and lightly syruped pancakes. This is my number-one go-to recipe, and what I love about it is that any leftover pancakes can be frozen and reheated on busy school mornings.

MAKES 16 FULL-SIZE OR ABOUT 36 SILVER-DOLLAR PANCAKES • TOTAL TIME: 1 HOUR

DIRECTIONS:

- In a medium bowl, combine the flour, baking powder, baking soda, salt, and sugar. Whisk to break up any clumps and make a well in the center.

- In a separate medium bowl, whisk together the eggs, buttermilk, butter, and vanilla. Pour this into the well in the dry ingredients and stir until just combined. A slightly lumpy batter is okay.

- Heat an electric griddle to 350°F or a skillet over medium to medium-high heat. (If I'm using a skillet, I always have to adjust between the two temperatures to get it just right, so keep a close eye on it.)

- Lightly oil the griddle (or skillet) with coconut oil. Scoop ¼ cup of the batter and pour it onto the griddle. I usually griddle four to six pancakes at a time. Cook for 3 to 4 minutes, or until the bottoms are dark golden and the air bubbles pop and no longer fill back in with batter, then flip and cook for 3 to 4 minutes on the second side. Repeat with the remaining batter. Serve immediately or keep them warm in a low oven while you make the rest.

INGREDIENTS:

2 cups unbleached all-purpose flour

1 teaspoon baking powder

½ teaspoon baking soda

½ teaspoon kosher salt

2 tablespoons sugar

2 large eggs, at room temperature

2¼ cups buttermilk, at room temperature

3 tablespoons unsalted butter, melted and cooled to room temperature

1 teaspoon pure vanilla extract

Coconut oil, for the griddle

SIMPLY SCRATCH TIP

I love to make a double batch of pancakes, freeze them, and reheat during the week for breakfast. Once the pancakes are cool, lay them in batches in a single layer on a parchment paper-lined baking sheet and freeze for 20 minutes. Now you can stack them, however many at a time, wrap them in heavy-duty aluminum foil, and freeze. They should last a month or two in the freezer. Who doesn't love insta-breakfast?

Lazy Weekend Yeasted Waffles

INGREDIENTS:

½ cup warm water (110 to 115°F)

1 tablespoon sugar

1 (¼-ounce) packet active dry yeast (2¼ teaspoons)

3 cups unbleached all-purpose flour

¾ teaspoon kosher salt

8 tablespoons (1 stick) unsalted butter, melted and cooled to room temperature

½ cup unsweetened applesauce

2 cups whole milk

2 large eggs

½ teaspoon baking soda

1 teaspoon pure vanilla extract

Coconut oil, for brushing the waffle iron

Room-temperature butter, for serving

Pure maple syrup, for serving

SIMPLY SCRATCH TIP

Extra waffles can be flash-frozen: just place them in a single layer on a baking sheet and freeze for 25 minutes, then package them up in freezer-safe containers or wrap tightly in aluminum foil. They'll keep for 2 to 3 months, and they reheat nicely because they can go straight from the freezer to the toaster.

I live for lazy weekends. Sleeping in, coffee in bed, and a breakfast I barely have to put any effort into is my idea of heaven. You can start this recipe the night before and finish the next morning—all you have to do is roll out of bed and turn on the waffle iron! Also, this easy recipe doesn't require you to whisk egg whites into submission until your arm falls off. Yeasted waffles are a fantastic way to make light and crispy waffles without a lot of work. Prep this recipe the night before and enjoy sleeping in!

MAKES 16 WAFFLES • TOTAL TIME: 15 MINUTES TO OVERNIGHT

DIRECTIONS:

- In a small bowl, stir together the warm water and sugar until the sugar has dissolved. Stir in the yeast and let it sit and proof for 10 minutes, or until foamy.

- In a very large bowl, whisk together the flour and salt. Pour in the yeast mixture, melted butter, applesauce, and milk. Using a hand mixer, whisk until smooth. Cover with plastic wrap and let stand at room temperature, where it will rise for 8 hours to overnight.

- When ready to cook, in a small bowl, beat together the eggs, baking soda, and vanilla with a fork. Pour the egg mixture into the batter and whisk to combine.

- Preheat a waffle maker and lightly grease the plates with coconut oil.

- Working in batches, pour about ⅓ cup of the batter into the waffle maker and cook until golden, 4 to 6 minutes.

- Serve immediately with butter and maple syrup.

VARIATION: Try adding fresh berries or lemon zest to the batter!

Cornbread

I have some weird magnetic pull to cornbread. I love it plain, with a little drizzle of honey or maple syrup, and especially crumbled and used in stuffing. There are endless add-ins you can use to take cornbread to the next level. Some of my favorites are crispy bacon, jalapeño, and even fresh herbs like sage. This cornbread is a good base to build upon. It's thick, hearty in texture, and truly a cinch to make. This recipe makes quite a bit but can easily be halved to make a smaller batch.

MAKES 24 SQUARES • TOTAL TIME: 35 MINUTES

DIRECTIONS:

- Preheat the oven to 425°F. Grease a 9 by 13-inch baking dish with 1 tablespoon of the butter and line it with parchment paper, allowing the extra paper to hang over the sides.

- In a large bowl, whisk together the flour, cornmeal, baking powder, baking soda, and salt. Make a well in the center and set aside.

- In a separate medium bowl, whisk together the buttermilk, eggs, remaining 8 tablespoons melted butter, and honey. While stirring gently with a wooden spoon, pour the egg mixture into the flour mixture and stir until just combined.

- Pour the cornbread batter into the prepared pan and smooth out the top with a spatula. Bake for 18 to 20 minutes, or until a toothpick inserted into the center comes out clean with a few crumbs attached. Rotate the pan halfway during baking to ensure even cooking.

- Let the cornbread cool in the pan for 15 to 20 minutes, then use the overhanging parchment paper to remove it from the pan and cut it into 24 portions.

- Serve warm with butter.

INGREDIENTS:

8 tablespoons (1 stick) unsalted butter, melted and cooled to room temperature, plus 1 tablespoon for the baking dish

2 cups unbleached all-purpose flour

2 cups medium-grind yellow cornmeal

2 tablespoons baking powder

1 teaspoon baking soda

1¼ teaspoons kosher salt

2 cups buttermilk

4 large eggs

2 tablespoons honey

SIMPLY SCRATCH TIP

Have leftover cornbread? Use it in my Cornbread & Leek Stuffed Pork Chops (page 228).

Sauces, Dressings & Dips

Spicy Southwest Dip

INGREDIENTS:

½ cup Homemade Mayonnaise
(page 25)

½ cup sour cream

1 teaspoon Adobo Seasoning
(page 38)

½ teaspoon paprika

½ teaspoon kosher salt

¼ teaspoon cayenne pepper

This dip is slightly spicy and majorly addicting. It requires little effort but can be served with vegetables or onion rings, or even used as a spread on just about any sandwich. Really, the options are pretty much endless. The only hard part about this recipe is having to wait ever so patiently while it magically transforms in the fridge. Longest wait ever, but totally worth it.

This dip is perfect for dipping potato chips, quesadillas, or Baked Parsnip Fries (page 163).

MAKES 1 CUP • TOTAL TIME: 1 HOUR

DIRECTIONS:

- In a small bowl, combine all the ingredients and stir until smooth. Cover and refrigerate for at least 1 hour before serving.

Herb Blue Cheese Dressing & Dip

Hi. My name is Laurie, and I'm addicted to blue cheese. But my love for the deliciously pungent stuff is only one reason that I can't get enough of this dressing. This dressing is a twofer. By playing with the sour cream and buttermilk ratios you can either pour it as a rich dressing over a Grilled Romaine "Wedge" Salad (page 143) or use it as a thick, satisfying dip for spicy hot wings (see variation below). And I absolutely love adding fresh herbs—it gives a bright earthiness to this already amazing dip.

MAKES 1½ CUPS • TOTAL TIME: 5 MINUTES PLUS 1 HOUR TO OVERNIGHT

DIRECTIONS:

- In a bowl, combine the mayonnaise, sour cream, buttermilk, vinegar, Worcestershire, parsley, and chives. Add the crumbled blue cheese, stir, and season with the salt and pepper. Cover and refrigerate for at least 1 hour, or until ready to serve.

VARIATION: To make a dip, decrease the buttermilk by ¼ cup.

INGREDIENTS:

½ cup Homemade Mayonnaise (page 25)

¼ cup sour cream

½ cup buttermilk

1 tablespoon white wine vinegar

A few splashes of Worcestershire sauce

2 tablespoons minced fresh flat-leaf parsley

2½ tablespoons chopped fresh chives

Heaping ½ cup crumbled blue cheese

½ teaspoon kosher salt

¼ teaspoon freshly ground black pepper

Warm Dijon Vinaigrette

This is one of those recipes that will make you glad you have that jar of bacon fat in the fridge. You'll want the unstrained bacon fat with all the delicious browned bits. Just scoop some into a skillet and you're on your way to making a tantalizing vinaigrette. This dressing is extremely versatile; it works wonders drizzled over a spinach salad or as a tangy addition to my Grilled Scallions with Dijon Vinaigrette (page 200). It's classy without being a total show-off, so your friends won't feel intimidated the next time you throw a dinner party. It's simple, yet tastes better than any vinaigrette you could possibly purchase at a store. Plus, it calls for bacon fat—I mean, hello?!

MAKES ¼ CUP • TOTAL TIME: 10 MINUTES

DIRECTIONS:

- In a medium skillet, melt the bacon fat over medium-low heat. Add the shallot and garlic and sauté until soft, 3 to 4 minutes. Reduce the heat to low and add the mustard, vinegar, salt, and pepper. Simmer for 2 minutes, then transfer to a heat-safe container.

- Serve immediately.

INGREDIENTS:

2 tablespoons unstrained bacon fat

1 tablespoon minced shallot

1 small clove garlic, passed through a garlic press

3 tablespoons Dijon mustard

2 tablespoons white wine vinegar

¼ teaspoon kosher salt

⅛ teaspoon coarsely ground black pepper

My Grandma's Greek Dressing

How could something so simple be so perfect? I've been asking myself this for years. This dressing has been the only Greek dressing I've used since my mom came over for dinner once toting a big fat Greek salad and a copy of this recipe. Only after I spent a good 15 minutes going on and *on* about how much I loved it did she tell me it was my grandmother's recipe. What makes it so special? Fresh lemon juice and garlic. Another key is to crush the oregano in the palm of your hand to release its aroma. Done deal.

MAKES ¾ CUP • TOTAL TIME: 10 MINUTES

DIRECTIONS:

- Pass the garlic through a garlic press into a glass jar or resealable storage container. Add the oregano, salt, and pepper. Pour in the lemon juice and olive oil.

- Shake. Pour. Swoon.

- Store the salad dressing in the refrigerator, but pull it out 10 to 15 minutes prior to using to warm up the solidified oil, or run the jar under warm tap water. Store in the refrigerator for 3 to 4 months.

INGREDIENTS:

1 large clove garlic

1 teaspoon dried oregano, crushed in your palm

½ teaspoon kosher salt

¼ teaspoon coarsely ground black pepper

¼ cup fresh lemon juice, strained of pulp and seeds

½ cup olive oil

SIMPLY SCRATCH TIP

This dressing also does double duty as a marinade in recipes like my Roasted Red Pepper, Sun-Dried Tomato & Feta Topped Chicken (page 217). Just be sure not to marinate too long, as the lemon juice can toughen the protein and slowly "cook" the chicken.

Buttermilk Ranch Dressing & Dip

¾ cup Homemade Mayonnaise (page 25)

½ cup sour cream

½ cup buttermilk

2 cloves garlic, minced

3 tablespoons snipped fresh chives

2 tablespoons minced fresh flat-leaf parsley

2 tablespoons minced fresh dill

1 teaspoon dried oregano, crushed in your palm

¼ teaspoon dried marjoram

¼ teaspoon paprika

Pinch of cayenne pepper (optional)

¾ teaspoon kosher salt

¼ teaspoon freshly ground black pepper

Pat and I have a thing about ranch dressing. It can't be too thick and it can't be too thin, either. In our expert opinions, there's a fine balance. That's why I love to make my own ranch dressing, because I get to determine the perfect texture. This ranch calls for a lot of fresh herbs—you will need to give it some time in the fridge to let the buttermilk permeate them and bring forth their natural flavor. When it's ready, you'll find yourself looking around for something, *anything*, to dunk into it. Vegetables, baked chicken tenders . . . a shoe?! Just kidding, that would not be good eats. Stick with salads, raw vegetables, and pizza. You can't go wrong with this ranch.

MAKES 2 CUPS • TOTAL TIME: 5 MINUTES PLUS 1 HOUR TO OVERNIGHT

DIRECTIONS:

- In a medium bowl, stir together the mayonnaise, sour cream, and buttermilk until smooth. Stir in the garlic, chives, parsley, dill, oregano, marjoram, paprika, cayenne, salt, and black pepper. Cover and refrigerate for 1 hour or up to overnight (the longer, the better!).

VARIATION: To make a dip, decrease the buttermilk to ¼ cup.

Pizza Sauce & Italian Sandwich Spread

Having made this sauce several dozen times, I can honestly say it's my favorite pizza sauce. I stumbled upon this recipe when I was making pizza one day and realized I didn't have any tomato sauce on hand. Relying on my inner *Chopped* skills, I resorted to using a can of tomato paste. Then I added layers of flavors using onion, spices, and sun-dried tomatoes. I thinned it out with wine and water and simmered it until thick and robust. And it was amazing.

Use this recipe as a sauce on your next pizza, or smear it on your favorite sandwich. It adds incredible flavor. Like most tomato-based recipes, it does benefit from a little time in the fridge, so if at all possible, make it a day or several hours in advance before using.

MAKES 1½ CUPS • TOTAL TIME: 30 MINUTES

DIRECTIONS:

- In a 10-inch skillet, heat the olive oil over medium heat. Add the onion and garlic and cook for 4 to 6 minutes, or until soft.

- Add the sun-dried tomatoes, oregano, and basil. Stir and cook for 1 minute; the oil and the heat of the pan will soften up the dried herbs. Pour in the wine and simmer until reduced by half.

- Add the tomato paste, sugar, and 1 cup water. Slowly stir until combined. Reduce the heat to low and simmer the sauce, uncovered, for 10 to 15 minutes. Season with the salt and pepper.

- Use immediately, or let the sauce cool slightly, then pour into a jar and let cool completely. Store in the refrigerator for up to 1 week.

INGREDIENTS:

1 tablespoon olive oil

½ cup minced white onion

2 cloves garlic, minced or passed through a garlic press

2 tablespoons minced sun-dried tomatoes (packed in olive oil)

2 teaspoons dried oregano, crushed in your palm

1½ teaspoons dried basil

2 tablespoons white wine (such as pinot grigio)

1 (6-ounce) can tomato paste

¼ teaspoon sugar

1 teaspoon kosher salt

¼ teaspoon coarsely ground black pepper

SIMPLY SCRATCH TIP

If you want to avoid cooking with alcohol, substitute an equal amount of chicken or vegetable broth for the wine.

Classic Marinara

INGREDIENTS:

1 tablespoon olive oil

2 large shallots, chopped (about ¾ cup)

3 cloves garlic, chopped

¼ cup good dry red wine (like merlot)

1 (28-ounce) can whole San Marzano tomatoes, pureed (3 cups)

1 (8-ounce) can tomato sauce

1¼ teaspoons kosher salt

½ teaspoon freshly ground black pepper

½ teaspoon sugar

Pinch of red pepper flakes

Whether it's poured over chicken Parmesan or used to simmer meatballs (like my Spaghetti & Meatballs, page 235), marinara sauce is a go-to recipe that should be in everyone's repertoire. In my opinion, the key to a good red sauce is using San Marzano tomatoes. They're somewhat similar to Roma tomatoes except they're narrower, with a thicker flesh, fewer seeds, and more flavor. I also prefer them because they tend to be less acidic. In a supermarket, you'll only find them peeled, whole, and in a can. You can easily turn them into sauce by whizzing them up in your food processor. If you want a little more tomato texture, crush them by hand for a more rustic and less refined sauce.

MAKES 3 CUPS • TOTAL TIME: 40 MINUTES

DIRECTIONS:

- In a 12-inch skillet, heat the olive oil over medium-low heat. Add the shallots and sauté for about 5 minutes, until soft. Add the garlic, stir, and continue to cook for 1 to 2 minutes more.

- Increase the heat to medium and pour in the wine, scraping up any brown bits from the bottom of the pan with a wooden spoon. Simmer and cook until reduced by three-quarters. Slowly add the pureed tomatoes, tomato sauce, salt, black pepper, sugar, and red pepper flakes.

- Reduce the heat to low and simmer for 25 minutes, or until the sauce has reduced by one-third.

SIMPLY SCRATCH TIP

If you would like to opt out of using wine in this recipe, try using chicken, beef, or vegetable broth instead.

Guacamole

My house is a revolving door for avocados. At least twice a week we make either this classic version of guacamole or my 5-Minute Avocado Spread (page 80). I fell in love with guac as a young teen when I finally decided to give it a try after avoiding it for years. (Did I mention I was a picky eater?) I would think to myself, *How can something* that *green possibly be any good?* But after one bite, I totally got it. Now, I eat it for lunch, as a snack, as an appetizer . . . whenever I can, pretty much. I'm so very proud of the fact that I've passed my love for avocados down to my daughters, too. I'm still working on my husband—he sort of likes them, but one day, he'll full-on love them, just like us.

This guacamole is everything a person or a chip could ask for.

MAKES ABOUT 4 CUPS • TOTAL TIME: 25 MINUTES

DIRECTIONS:

- Halve the avocados, remove and discard the pits, and scoop the flesh into a large bowl. Add the lime juice, garlic, red onion, cilantro, and salt and use a potato masher to combine to your desired texture. Serve immediately.

VARIATION: For a loaded version, try adding chopped tomato, ¾ cup grated sharp cheddar cheese, crumbled crispy bacon, and ½ teaspoon cayenne pepper for a subtle back-of-the-throat heat kick.

INGREDIENTS:

4 large ripe avocados

Juice of 1 lime (about 2 tablespoons)

2 cloves garlic, minced

⅓ cup diced red onion

⅓ cup fresh cilantro leaves, chopped

1 teaspoon kosher salt

SIMPLY SCRATCH TIP

I store my guac in an airtight container, but first I press a piece of plastic wrap against the guacamole to keep it from touching as much air as possible. Air + avocados = oxidation (translation: it will turn an unappetizing brown color). Even though the lime juice aids in locking in that bright green color, the plastic wrap acts as an insurance policy. You can also spread a thin layer of mayonnaise over the surface. It may seem strange, but it works and won't change the taste of the guacamole.

5-Minute Avocado Spread

1 clove garlic

2 ripe avocados

Juice of ½ lime

½ teaspoon kosher salt

Got two avocados (and garlic and a little lime juice) and five minutes? You can make this super-fast and ultra-creamy avocado dip. In our house, we use it as a dip for chips and top our tacos and fajitas with it, and it also works mighty fine as a spread on a turkey BLT . . . really any and all sandwiches, to be exact.

This velvety-smooth dip is all made in a mini food processor, so you can have it ready and in your mouth in record time.

DIRECTIONS:

- In the bowl of a mini food processor, pulse the garlic until finely chopped. Halve the avocados, remove and discard the pits, and scoop the flesh into the food processor. Add the lime juice and salt and process until smooth.

- Serve right away or press plastic wrap onto the top of the spread to keep it from oxidizing.

Pico de Gallo

I make pico *a lot* in the summer months, when fresh produce is at its prime and I have the majority of the ingredients growing in my garden and at my fingertips. It's easily one of the most versatile condiments. Not only is this pico great for scooping onto your tortilla chips and tacos, but it's also delicious as a topping to my Broiled Chili-Lime-Crusted Tilapia (page 249) or as yet another wonderful condiment for Skirt Steak Fajitas (page 233).

MAKES ABOUT 2 CUPS • TOTAL TIME: 20 MINUTES

DIRECTIONS:

- In a medium bowl, combine the tomatoes, red onion, scallions, cilantro, jalapeño, and garlic. Add the lime juice and oil, season with the salt, and stir to combine.

- Serve immediately or cover with plastic wrap and refrigerate until ready to serve.

INGREDIENTS:

3 plum (Roma) tomatoes, seeded and diced

⅓ cup finely diced red onion

2 scallions, sliced

2 tablespoons chopped fresh cilantro

1 tablespoon minced jalapeño

1 teaspoon minced garlic

Juice of ½ lime

1 teaspoon olive oil

½ teaspoon kosher salt

Dressinades

Dressing + Marinade = Dressinade. So, yes, dressinade is totally a made-up word. It means what you think it does: a salad dressing that can also work as a marinade. When I first coined the word, it was a joke, but then the name just sort of stuck. Silly as it may sound, life's so much easier when you have homemade dressinades around. If you have left-over unused dressinade still in the jar? Pop it back into the fridge and pour it over tomorrow's salad with dinner. Have a cup of dressinade you need to use before the end of the week? Marinate chicken breasts or steak for 1 hour and grill it up! These are my favorite kinds of recipes: two birds, one stone, and all that.

Balsamic Herb Dressinade

MAKES 1 ½ CUPS • TOTAL TIME: 35 MINUTES

DIRECTIONS:

- In a 1-pint glass jar, combine all the ingredients. Secure the lid and shake until combined. Let stand for 30 minutes before using.

- Store any unused dressing in the refrigerator. If the oil solidifies, run the sealed jar under warm water and shake well before using.

- If you're using fresh herbs, this dressinade will last for 1 to 2 weeks in the refrigerator. Dried herbs will give it a longer shelf life of 2 to 3 months.

INGREDIENTS:

2 cloves garlic, minced

1 tablespoon chopped fresh basil, or 1 teaspoon dried

2 teaspoons chopped fresh rosemary, or 1 teaspoon dried

1 teaspoon chopped fresh thyme, or ½ teaspoon dried

¾ teaspoon kosher salt

¼ teaspoon coarsely ground black pepper

2 teaspoons Dijon mustard

6 tablespoons balsamic vinegar

2 tablespoons red wine vinegar

1 cup grape-seed oil or olive oil

Italian Dressinade

INGREDIENTS:

2 cloves garlic, minced

1 small shallot, minced (about 2 tablespoons)

1 teaspoon dried basil

1 teaspoon dried oregano

¾ teaspoon kosher salt

½ teaspoon freshly ground black pepper

¼ teaspoon red pepper flakes (optional)

¼ cup red wine vinegar

½ cup olive oil

MAKES 1 CUP • TOTAL TIME: 15 MINUTES

DIRECTIONS:

- In a 1-pint glass jar, combine all the ingredients. Tightly secure the lid and shake to combine.

- Store any unused dressing in the refrigerator for up to 3 months. If the oil solidifies, run the sealed jar under warm water and shake well before using.

SIMPLY SCRATCH TIP

For a creamy version, try adding a couple of tablespoons of mayonnaise.

Compound Butters

Coming up with flavored butter combinations has become a minor obsession of mine! Compound butters are a delicious way to get creative with butter. I love to make fruit butters to top waffles, toast, or scones. Savory butters are wonderful on Grilled Rib-Eye Steaks with Mushroom-Shallot Butter (page 238) or melted over cooked vegetables. Here are a few of my favorites to spread on biscuits, sauté with your favorite vegetables, spread over corn on the cob, top a finished salmon fillet, or lather up chicken before baking (see page 86). Because everything can be better with a little butter.

Strawberry-Cinnamon Sugar Compound Butter

This is delicious on freshly made waffles, toast, or pastries.

DIRECTIONS:

- In the bowl of a mini food processor, combine the butter, cinnamon, and sugar. Add in strawberries and pulse until combined. Use immediately or refrigerate until ready to serve. Allow the butter to soften by removing it from the refrigerator 30 minutes prior to using.

INGREDIENTS:

8 tablespoons (1 stick) salted butter, at room temperature

½ teaspoon ground cinnamon

2 tablespoons sugar

⅓ cup hulled and diced strawberries

Jalapeño-Honey Compound Butter

9 tablespoons (1 stick plus 1 tablespoon) salted butter, at room temperature

1 jalapeño, seeded and diced

1 clove garlic, minced

1 tablespoon honey

Try this on freshly grilled corn or slathered over cornbread or biscuits.

DIRECTIONS:

• In a small skillet, melt 1 tablespoon of the butter. Add the jalapeño and garlic and cook until softened. Let cool completely. In the bowl of a mini food processor, combine the honey and remaining 8 tablespoons of butter, blending until smooth. Add in the jalapeño-garlic mixture and pulse to combine. Use immediately or refrigerate until ready to serve. Allow the butter to soften by removing it from the refrigerator 30 minutes prior to using.

Lemon, Garlic & Herb Compound Butter

INGREDIENTS:

8 tablespoons (1 stick) salted butter, at room temperature

Zest of 1 lemon

2 cloves garlic, minced

2 tablespoons chopped fresh flat-leaf parsley

Leaves from 1 sprig fresh thyme, chopped (about ½ teaspoon)

Perfect on top of veggies or seafood, or to rub over chicken before cooking.

DIRECTIONS:

• In a medium bowl, stir together all the ingredients with a wooden spoon or spatula. Use immediately or refrigerate until ready to serve. Allow the butter to soften by removing it from the refrigerator 30 minutes prior to using.

Romesco Sauce

Romesco is more than just a sauce. It's a robust condiment that can be served over grilled meat, spread over toasted baguette slices, or generously spooned over vegetables (it's what gives my Vegetarian Polenta Skillet, page 101, a level-up flavor boost). I make my romesco by roasting halved Roma tomatoes and garlic, then blitzing those with toasted almonds, stale bread, and other seasonings. Think of it as a roasted tomato pesto of a sort. The flavor is nothing short of WOW.

MAKES 2 CUPS • TOTAL TIME: 1 HOUR

DIRECTIONS:

- Preheat the oven to 400°F.

- Arrange the tomato halves cut-side up on a rimmed baking sheet. Drizzle with 1 tablespoon of the olive oil and season with ½ teaspoon of the salt and the pepper.

- Break up the head of garlic and place all but one of the unpeeled garlic cloves in the center of a piece of heavy-duty aluminum foil. Drizzle with 1 teaspoon of the olive oil, then fold and crimp up the sides of the foil so the garlic is secure in a foil package.

- Place the foil package on the baking sheet with the tomatoes and roast for 25 minutes. Remove the foil pouch and let cool for 10 minutes, or until safe to handle. Roast the tomatoes for 20 minutes more.

- Once the roasted garlic cloves are cool, remove the skin and place the flesh in the bowl of a food processor. Add the reserved clove of raw garlic, remaining 2 tablespoons olive oil, the roasted tomatoes, almonds, bread, chili powder, vinegar, and remaining 1 teaspoon salt and process until smooth.

- Serve immediately or store in an airtight container in the refrigerator until ready to use. This sauce will keep for 1 to 2 weeks.

INGREDIENTS:

6 large plum (Roma) tomatoes, halved horizontally

3 tablespoons plus 1 teaspoon olive oil

1½ teaspoons kosher salt

½ teaspoon coarsely ground black pepper

1 small head garlic

⅓ cup blanched almonds, toasted

1 thick slice stale sturdy bread (like sourdough), torn into pieces

¾ teaspoon chili powder

2 tablespoons red wine vinegar

SIMPLY SCRATCH TIP

Roasting the tomatoes softens the skin so you do not have to peel them. Just throw them in with the skin, seeds and all. Feel free to substitute toasted bread for stale bread if you don't have any on hand.

Chimichurri Sauce

INGREDIENTS:

6 cloves garlic

Leaves from 1 large bunch fresh flat-leaf parsley (about 2 cups)

3 tablespoons white wine vinegar

Juice of 1 medium lemon

1 teaspoon kosher salt

⅛ to ¼ teaspoon cayenne pepper

¾ cup olive oil

The first time chimichurri graced my taste buds, it was love at first bite. My sister used it as a marinade for flank steak, and we feasted on the most amazing fajitas I've ever had the pleasure of eating. Essentially, chimichurri is a condiment made up of fresh parsley, olive oil, and lots of fresh garlic. Lots and lots of fresh garlic. Since that fateful encounter, I've used it as an additional topping to my burgers, as a condiment for deliciously charred grilled rib-eye, and—my personal fave—Smashed Cast-Iron Skillet Potatoes with Chimichurri (page 184).

MAKES 1 CUP • TOTAL TIME: 10 MINUTES

DIRECTIONS:

- In the bowl of a food processor, pulse the garlic to coarsely chop. Add the parsley, vinegar, lemon juice, salt, cayenne, and olive oil. Process until just combined.

- Keep refrigerated until ready to serve. Chimichurri will keep for 1 to 2 weeks in the refrigerator.

CHAPTER THREE

Breakfast & Brunch

Oh, breakfast—it's the meal that starts the day, and a good day always begins with a breakfast that's wholesome and, most important, filling. Breakfast food is probably my favorite, but then again, it's hard to choose. . . . There is just something about a stack of pancakes soaked with butter and dripping with maple syrup, or a plate of crispy home fries topped with a perfect fried egg—with its even more perfect drippy yolk—that just starts the day off right.

When I was growing up, there wasn't a single box of sugared cereal, toaster pastries, or instant oatmeal in our pantry. None whatsoever. My mom was the health food enforcer, so when it came to breakfast, it was either a slice of peanut butter (and grape jelly!) toast or a bowl of oatmeal with a small sprinkle of dark brown sugar. In a nutshell, highly processed foods were something I never did see too much of.

My mom always encouraged us to cook in the kitchen, and breakfast was one of the first things I tackled. I learned how to make most simple breakfast dishes before I was out of elementary school: oatmeal, pancakes, French toast, and even the all-time classic egg-in-the-hole. My mom taught me well.

Today, breakfast in our house isn't much different than it was when I was growing up. I don't buy sugared cereals unless it's a special occasion (everything in moderation, right?). Oatmeal still isn't "instant," and toast, well, that happens at all times of day, not just during breakfast. . . . But Sundays are the day my family and I make breakfast really shine. We cook everything from Baked Cinnamon Sugar Rum-Raisin French Toast to Sausage Gravy over Buttermilk Biscuits to my personal favorite: the classic fried eggs on top of Breakfast Home Fries (with a side of bacon, of course). Sunday family breakfast has become our own little tradition. It's something we all look forward to every single weekend: having breakfast, and making memories.

I have to say, if there's one thing that I love just as much as breakfast, it would definitely be brunch. Combine sleeping in with all-things breakfast and all-things lunch? Pure genius, if you ask me. Dishes like fried egg BLT waffles, scones, and/or roasted banana on anything is what brunch is all about. Anything goes. You could have something sweet, or savory, or both.

In my mind, the only way that breakfast or brunch could get any better is if it were served to me in bed. With a steaming cup of fresh coffee. Obviously.

Breakfast & Brunch

Tomato, Spinach & Parmesan Baked Eggs

In our house, we like our eggs when the whites and yolk are set and you can eat them on thick slices of buttered toast. Because, frankly, who needs a fork when you have toasted and buttered ciabatta? (I kid. Sort of.) After one bite you'll be thinking about these baked eggs for days, I tell you.

Whether you're feeding a large crew or just need to whip up breakfast for yourself, this wholesome meal is your jam. It can easily be scaled up or down depending on what you need, and is virtually effortless (which is music to my ears first thing in the morning). It's guaranteed to leave you full and satisfied. All that's left afterward is to wash the dishes. Okay, pretend I didn't just say that.

SERVES 4 • TOTAL TIME: 30 MINUTES

DIRECTIONS:

- Preheat the oven to 375°F. Spray four shallow-sided oval baking dishes with olive oil or cooking spray and place on a rimmed baking sheet.

- In a small bowl, combine the Parmesan, parsley, and thyme. Set aside.

- In a small saucepan, melt the butter with the garlic and cook for 1 to 2 minutes, or until the garlic has softened.

- Place the spinach, tomatoes, and red pepper flakes in a large bowl. Pour the garlic butter over the top and toss to coat. Divide the tomato mixture among the prepared baking dishes, season with a pinch of salt and black pepper, and bake for 10 minutes.

- Working quickly, crack two eggs into a measuring cup and carefully pour them into one baking dish over the tomato mixture. Repeat with the remaining eggs so each baking dish is topped with two eggs. Sprinkle some of the Parmesan-herb mixture over each baking dish, dividing it evenly.

INGREDIENTS:

Olive oil mister or cooking spray

3 tablespoons freshly grated Parmesan cheese

2 teaspoons minced fresh flat-leaf parsley

½ teaspoon minced fresh thyme leaves

3 tablespoons unsalted butter

1 clove garlic, minced

4 cups baby spinach

1 cup halved cherry tomatoes

½ teaspoon red pepper flakes

Kosher salt and freshly ground black pepper

8 medium or large eggs, at room temperature (see Simply Scratch Tip)

Buttered toast, for serving

- Return the baking sheet with the baking dishes to the oven, setting it on the lowest rack, and bake for 12 to 15 minutes more, or until the egg whites are opaque and the yolks are cooked to your preference. Rotate the pans halfway during baking to ensure even cooking.

- Serve warm with buttered toast.

SIMPLY SCRATCH TIP

To bring your eggs up to room temperature, place them in a bowl and cover with warm (not hot) water. Leave them for about 15 minutes while you prep breakfast.

Buckwheat Pancakes

As a kid, if pancakes were on the morning menu, ten times out of ten my mother made them with buckwheat flour. I never could refuse a plate of these deeply brown cakes, each one smeared with copious amounts of butter and soaked through with maple syrup. I didn't know anyone made pancakes with white flour only until much later in life. And it never fails that whenever I make these pancakes, I'm instantly transported to my childhood kitchen table with a knife and fork in each hand.

While it's true that buckwheat flour adds nutritional value to these pancakes (which is a good thing!), it's really the earthy and wholesome flavor that I've come to love. To brighten up these folksy pancakes, I like to add a little orange juice to the batter and then finish off my towering stack with a generous amount of sliced fresh strawberries tossed in a little brown sugar. Don't worry, I still drizzle a little (okay, a lot of) maple syrup over the top as well.

These griddle cakes are a nod to my mom. She made them for me, and now I make them for my girls. I hope that they, too, will pass this recipe down to their children, and so on, for generations to come. It's definitely a nostalgic recipe for my family.

MAKES 18 PANCAKES • TOTAL TIME: 40 MINUTES

DIRECTIONS:

- Heat an electric griddle to 375ºF or a skillet over medium-high heat.

- In a large bowl, whisk together both flours, the sugar, baking powder, baking soda, and salt. Set aside.

- In a medium bowl, whisk together the milk, orange juice, eggs, and vanilla. While whisking slowly, pour the milk mixture and the melted coconut oil into the flour mixture and whisk until just combined.

INGREDIENTS:

1 ½ cups buckwheat flour

½ cup unbleached all-purpose flour

2 tablespoons sugar

2 teaspoons baking powder

½ teaspoon baking soda

1 teaspoon salt

2 cups whole milk

¼ cup fresh orange juice

2 large eggs

1 teaspoon pure vanilla extract

3 tablespoons coconut oil, melted, plus more for the griddle

Butter and pure maple syrup, for serving

- Place 1 teaspoon of coconut oil onto the hot griddle; use a spatula to spread it around until it has melted and the griddle is evenly coated. Working in batches, measure ¼ cup of pancake batter and pour it onto the hot griddle. Cook the pancakes for 4 minutes or until bubbles form, break, and do not fill back in, then flip. Cook the pancakes on the second side for 30 seconds to 1 minute.

- Repeat with the rest of the pancake batter, adding more coconut oil to the griddle only as needed.

- Serve warm with butter and real maple syrup.

VARIATION: Try adding fresh fruit like bananas or berries into the pancake batter for extra healthy goodness.

SIMPLY SCRATCH TIP

I place the hot griddle cakes on a rimmed baking sheet and keep them warm in a preheated 200°F oven. No one likes cold pancakes. No one.

Sausage Gravy over Buttermilk Biscuits

INGREDIENTS:

1¼ pounds ground pork

1½ teaspoons rubbed sage

2 teaspoons kosher salt

¾ teaspoon freshly ground black pepper

½ teaspoon dried marjoram

¼ to ½ teaspoon red pepper flakes

1 teaspoon light brown sugar

⅓ cup unbleached all-purpose flour

2½ cups whole milk or half-and-half

12 Buttermilk Biscuits (page 62), warmed

I made the same sausage gravy for what felt like eons. Biscuits and gravy was quite often the dish I made for my family's Sunday breakfast feasts at home. Preparing it was as simple as buying and cooking up a roll of seasoned breakfast sausage and mixing in a little flour, milk, salt, and pepper.

This past year, though, I wanted to take my sausage gravy a step further. I started tinkering with making my own breakfast sausage, with the exception of grinding my own pork (because I just don't have patience for that noise, nor do I own a meat grinder, for that matter . . .) and wouldn't you know, I like this recipe better. This recipe is cozy on a plate, and my family can't get enough. For best results, make the sausage the night before.

P.S. Like a little spice? Consider upping the red pepper flakes for a spicier sausage gravy.

SERVES 6 • TOTAL TIME: 5 MINUTES PLUS OVERNIGHT

DIRECTIONS:

- **THE NIGHT BEFORE:** In the bowl of a stand mixer fitted with the paddle attachment, combine the pork, sage, 1 teaspoon of the salt, ½ teaspoon of the black pepper, the marjoram, red pepper flakes, and sugar. Mix until thoroughly combined. Cover the bowl with plastic wrap and refrigerate overnight.

- **THE MORNING OF:** Heat a 12-inch skillet over medium heat. Add the sausage meat and cook until browned. Sprinkle in the flour, stirring until the rendered fat has absorbed it all. Pour in the milk and bring to a simmer. Cook, stirring occasionally, for 10 to 15 minutes, or until the gravy has thickened.

- Season with the remaining 1 teaspoon salt and ¼ teaspoon black pepper before spooning over warm buttermilk biscuits.

Vegetarian Polenta Skillet

There's this quaint and cozy restaurant about fifteen minutes from where I live. Every time I go there for breakfast, I order the same exact thing: their insanely delicious breakfast polenta skillet. No lie. It's served in a screaming-hot cast-iron skillet; inside, there is cubed polenta topped with vegetables, romesco sauce, cheese, and two fried eggs—how good does that sound? Eventually, I decided I wanted to try to re-create my beloved breakfast from this restaurant at home. So I did, but I served it family-style in a giant skillet. (Eggs are optional but highly recommended.)

Making homemade polenta only takes a few minutes, and while it's cooling, the vegetables cook up fast in a hot skillet. Then you add the homemade romesco sauce and generously sprinkle the dish with Vermont white cheddar. Slide it under the broiler for a few minutes until the top is bubbling and brown and you have a little slice of heaven for your morning. With or without eggs, this flavorful breakfast can be on the table in under an hour, and is best served with thick slices of buttered toast.

SERVES 4 TO 6 • TOTAL TIME: 45 MINUTES

DIRECTIONS:

- Line an 8 by 11-inch rimmed baking sheet with aluminum foil and lightly grease the foil with butter or olive oil. Prepare the polenta as directed on page 199, but omit the cheddar cheese. Immediately pour the polenta into the prepared pan. With a spatula, spread it evenly and let it sit for 25 minutes, then invert the pan onto a cutting board. Peel off the foil and cut the polenta into 1-inch cubes. Set aside.

- Position the oven rack in the top portion of oven, crack the door, and heat the broiler on high.

- Melt 2 tablespoons of the butter in a 12-inch cast-iron skillet over medium-high heat. Add the zucchini, yellow squash, onion, and bell pepper and season with the salt and pepper.

INGREDIENTS:

Butter or olive oil, for the baking sheet

1 recipe Cheesy Polenta (page 199)

3 tablespoons unsalted butter

1 small zucchini, quartered and cut into ¼-inch pieces (about 2 cups)

1 small yellow squash, quartered and cut into ¼-inch pieces (about 2 cups)

1 cup chopped red onion

1 cup chopped red bell pepper

¾ teaspoon kosher salt, plus more as needed

¼ teaspoon coarsely ground black pepper, plus more as needed

1 cup Romesco Sauce (page 87)

4 ounces sharp Vermont cheddar cheese, grated

Fresh parsley or basil leaves, torn, for garnish

4 to 6 large eggs, for serving (optional)

Toss to coat the vegetables in the butter and then spread in an even layer. Let the vegetables cook undisturbed for 3 to 4 minutes, or until they start to turn a deep golden color. Stir and continue to cook until tender but still firm, 6 to 8 minutes more.

- Transfer the vegetables to a medium bowl and stir in the romesco sauce.

- Melt the remaining 1 tablespoon butter in the now empty skillet. Arrange the polenta cubes in an even layer in the skillet. Spoon the vegetable mixture over the top. Sprinkle with the grated cheddar and slide the skillet under the broiler for 2 to 4 minutes, or until the cheese is completely melted and lightly golden brown.

- Season with pepper and sprinkle with fresh parsley or basil.

- If desired, while the polenta is in the oven, heat a little olive oil or bacon fat in a skillet over medium heat. Crack in a few eggs at a time, sprinkle with salt and pepper, and cook until the whites are set. Flip and cook for a few seconds, depending on how you prefer your yolks.

- Serve immediately as is, or spoon onto plates and top with a fried egg.

SIMPLY SCRATCH TIP

To save time, I make my romesco sauce a few days in advance and keep it in the fridge until the morning of. Then I just pull it out when I start making the polenta, to take the chill off. Making the sauce in advance cuts down the prep time for this recipe immensely.

Breakfast Home Fries

INGREDIENTS:

4 medium russet potatoes, unpeeled, cut into 1-inch cubes

1 medium yellow onion, diced

1 tablespoon All-Purpose Seasoned Salt (page 38)

½ teaspoon garlic powder

¼ teaspoon coarsely ground black pepper

⅛ teaspoon cayenne pepper

3 to 4 tablespoons olive oil

2 tablespoons snipped fresh chives

I could make these blindfolded, turned backward, and in the pitch dark. THEY'RE THAT EASY. So that certainly means *anyone* can make them. The only hard part is deciding whether to top them with a fried egg (have you noticed that I'm always debating adding an egg?), stuff them into a burrito, or simply eat them straight from the pan. It's all possible with these gloriously crispy home fries.

SERVES 4 • TOTAL TIME: 40 MINUTES

DIRECTIONS:

• Preheat the oven to 400ºF.

• In a large bowl, combine the potatoes, onions, seasoned salt, garlic powder, black pepper, cayenne, and olive oil. Toss to coat the vegetables completely.

• Spread the potatoes in an even layer on two rimmed baking sheets and bake for 20 minutes. Rotate the baking sheets (do not attempt to flip the potatoes) and continue to bake for 8 to 10 minutes more, or until a fork pierces a potato easily. Remove and let the potatoes cool on the baking sheets for 5 minutes. This gives the potatoes time to release themselves from the bottom of the baking sheets.

• Sprinkle with snipped chives, toss to combine, and serve immediately.

Apricot & Toasted Almond Muesli

I will be the first to raise my hand and say that Monday through Friday, I'm the absolute worst at making myself breakfast. Coffee is a morning must-have, but I usually wait until the afternoon to eat my first real meal. Having a container of this nutrition-packed muesli lying around is a great way to make sure I have something healthy and filling to munch on first thing in the morning. It's also the perfect light midday snack that my kids and I all enjoy.

MAKES 8 CUPS • TOTAL TIME: 25 MINUTES

DIRECTIONS:

- Heat a dry 10-inch skillet over medium-low heat. Add the coconut flakes and toast, stirring often, until golden, 4 to 5 minutes. Transfer to a large bowl.

- In the same skillet, toast the almonds until golden and fragrant, 5 to 6 minutes. Transfer to the bowl with the coconut. Wipe out any small remaining pieces so they do not burn.

- Finally, in the same skillet, toast the wheat germ, flaxseeds, and sesame seeds, stirring often, for 3 to 4 minutes, until fragrant. Transfer to the bowl with the coconut and almonds and add the apricots, raisins, pepitas, sugar, sunflower seeds, and oats. Stir until combined, breaking up any large clumps of sugar.

- In a small cereal bowl, measure out 1/3 cup of the muesli. Top with fresh fruit and 1/4 to 1/3 cup almond milk, yogurt, or kefir.

- Serve immediately. For an extra burst of sweetness, serve with fresh fruit or berries.

INGREDIENTS:

1 cup unsweetened flaked coconut

1 cup coarsely chopped almonds

1/4 cup wheat germ

1/4 cup ground golden flaxseeds

2 tablespoons sesame seeds

1 cup chopped dried apricots

1/2 cup raisins

1/3 cup roasted pepitas

1/4 cup packed dark brown sugar

1/4 cup dry-roasted sunflower seeds

4 cups old-fashioned oats

Unsweetened vanilla almond milk, yogurt, or kefir, for serving

In-season fresh fruit or berries, for serving

Baked Cinnamon Sugar
Rum-Raisin French Toast

INGREDIENTS:

1 tablespoon unsalted butter

½ cup raisins

⅓ cup dark rum

6 large eggs

1⅓ cups whole milk

⅔ cup light coconut milk

½ cup granulated sugar

1 teaspoon pure vanilla extract

¼ teaspoon kosher salt

10 to 12 thick slices of bread (like French or sourdough)

1½ teaspoons ground cinnamon

2 tablespoons browned butter (see page 18)

½ cup pure maple syrup

Powdered sugar, for dusting

This recipe is exactly how French toast should be, in my book . . . deliciously simple, and yet the special touches like rum-plumped raisins and brown butter maple syrup make it perfect for a casual weekend breakfast or a special brunch.

I recommend pulling the ingredients together and making this the night before. Cover tightly with plastic wrap and refrigerate the entire dish overnight. Simply pull it out 30 minutes before sliding it into a preheated oven to bake.

In the meantime, enjoy the comforting smell of cinnamon and sugar as it works its way throughout your kitchen.

P.S. I call the corner piece.

MAKES 10 TO 12 SLICES • TOTAL TIME: 20 MINUTES TO 2 HOURS OR OVERNIGHT

DIRECTIONS:

· Butter a 9 by 13-inch baking dish.

· Place the raisins, rum, and 2 tablespoons water in a small saucepan and bring to a simmer over medium heat. Remove from the heat and set aside to let the raisins soak for 10 to 15 minutes, until plump.

· Meanwhile, in a large bowl, beat the eggs, milk, coconut milk, ¼ cup of the granulated sugar, the vanilla, and the salt.

· Dip one bread slice at a time into the egg mixture and arrange them in the prepared baking dish. Drain the raisins, scatter them over the bread, and pour any remaining egg mixture over the top. Cover tightly with plastic wrap and refrigerate for 2 hours or up to overnight.

· When ready to bake, preheat the oven to 375ºF and remove the plastic wrap.

- In a small bowl, combine the remaining ¼ cup granulated sugar and the cinnamon and sprinkle over the top. Cover the baking dish with aluminum foil and bake for 25 minutes. Remove the foil and bake for 20 minutes more.

- Combine the browned butter and maple syrup in a small saucepan over low heat until warm, 5 to 8 minutes. Serve the baked French toast on plates with a dusting of powdered sugar and a drizzle of warm brown butter maple syrup.

Lemon-Ginger Scones

This is the part where I confess that I once ate a whole batch of these scones in a record three days. I was testing the recipe and poof! They were gone. I didn't mean to, but do we ever? For me, a scone served with a steaming cup of coffee or tea is perfection. I haven't looked back since I was first introduced to scones by my friend Nichole, and this recipe does not disappoint.

These scones are inspired by some I love at a bakery in a nearby town. A quintessential classic American bakery complete with exposed brick walls and a hodgepodge collection of cute tables and chairs, this place serves the most amazing breads and baked goods. Ever. It's safe to say I've tried one of all their scones, and the lemon ginger are my number one favorite.

These scones are lemony, with a subtle ginger flair, and are topped with a thick layer of powdered sugar. What's not to love? So naturally when I tried them at home I ate them all. The end.

NOTE: The key to any good scone recipe is using ice-cold ingredients, so I cube the butter and keep it in the freezer, and keep everything else, with the exception of the dry ingredients, measured and combined in the fridge until I'm ready to mix them in.

MAKES 8 SCONES • TOTAL TIME: 30 MINUTES

DIRECTIONS:

- Preheat the oven to 400°F. Line a rimmed baking sheet with a silicone baking mat or parchment paper.

- In a 2-cup liquid measuring cup, use a fork to beat together the heavy cream, eggs, lemon extract, and vanilla until combined. Chill until ready to use.

- In a large bowl, combine the flour, sugar, baking powder, and salt. Drop in the ice-cold butter and use a pastry cutter to

INGREDIENTS:

½ cup cold heavy cream

2 large eggs

1 teaspoon organic lemon extract

½ teaspoon pure vanilla extract

2¼ cups unbleached all-purpose flour, plus more for dusting

3 tablespoons granulated sugar

1 tablespoon baking powder

¼ teaspoon kosher salt

¾ cup (1½ sticks) ice-cold unsalted butter, cut into cubes

¼ cup finely diced candied ginger

2 tablespoons grated lemon zest

¼ cup powdered sugar

cut the butter into the flour mixture until it resembles coarse wet sand.

- Pour in the chilled cream mixture, ginger, and lemon zest and use a rubber spatula to stir until just combined.

- Turn out the dough onto a lightly floured work surface and knead it a few times before forming it into a ball. With floured fingers, flatten it out into a 1½-inch-thick round. Cut the round into 8 equal-size wedges and transfer them to the prepared baking sheet.

- Bake for 15 to 18 minutes, rotating the baking sheet halfway through baking. Transfer the baked scones to a wire rack to cool. Once the scones have cooled, dust generously with powdered sugar before serving.

Heirloom Tomato Tart

This is a special brunch dish I wouldn't regret serving myself a generous (read: greedy) slice of. I wouldn't mind the dirty looks or the snickering comments about me being selfish, or worry about the extra calories—not one bit. Because when a homemade buttery pie crust is spread with a garlicky, whipped feta cream cheese, then topped with capers, chives, thin slices of heirloom tomatoes, and even more cheese (if you can believe it) and baked until golden . . . it's worth any hardship.

This tart is rustic yet fancy. It's also easy to make but looks as if it took you all day long to do. (Those are the *best* kind of recipes, right?) I'd definitely recommend serving it to your friends to impress them. You could even flick a little flour onto your face so people think you've just conquered a beast of a recipe in the kitchen. It'll be our secret; I promise I'll never tell.

SERVES 6 TO 8 • TOTAL TIME: 90 MINUTES

DIRECTIONS:

- Preheat the oven to 450ºF.

- Slice the tomatoes ⅛ to ¼ inch thick and arrange them on a clean kitchen towel or paper towel while you prepare the pie crust.

- Roll out the pie dough until it is ¼ inch thick and 10 inches in diameter. Drape it over a 9-inch round tart pan. Gently press the dough into the corners, then roll a rolling pin over the top edge to cut off the excess dough. Place the tart pan on a rimmed baking sheet and prick the dough a few times with a fork or gently line the dough with aluminum. Fill it with pie weights (if you don't have pie weights, use dried beans instead) and prebake the crust for 10 minutes. Remove from the oven and let cool for 20 minutes. Reduce the oven temperature to 375ºF.

- Meanwhile, in the bowl of a mini food processor, pulse the garlic cloves until minced. Add the feta and cream cheese

INGREDIENTS

4 large heirloom tomatoes

1 recipe All-Purpose Pie Crust (1 disc; page 49)

2 cloves garlic

4 ounces crumbled feta cheese

4 ounces cream cheese

4 tablespoons snipped fresh chives

2 tablespoons rinsed capers, coarsely chopped

¼ teaspoon kosher salt

¼ teaspoon coarsely ground black pepper

¼ cup plain Greek yogurt or whole milk regular yogurt

½ cup grated mozzarella cheese

1 tablespoon sliced fresh basil

2 tablespoons grated Parmesan cheese

2 teaspoons olive oil

and process until smooth. With an offset spatula, gently smear the whipped feta over the bottom of the cooled tart crust. Sprinkle with 2 tablespoons of the chives and the capers. Arrange the sliced tomatoes in three layers to fit in the tart pan. Season with the salt and pepper, then sprinkle with the remaining 2 tablespoons chives.

- In a small bowl, combine the yogurt, mozzarella, and basil. Stir and place small spoonfuls over the tomatoes and gently spread it evenly before sprinkling the Parmesan evenly over the top.

- Drizzle with the olive oil and bake for 40 to 45 minutes, or until the cheese is golden brown.

- Remove the tart from the oven and let cool for 15 to 20 minutes before slicing and serving.

SIMPLY SCRATCH TIP

When you lay the tomatoes out on a kitchen towel, it will absorb some of the moisture from the tomatoes. If possible, remove any of the gooey seeds before arranging them in the tart. You can cut some in half to fit, if need be.

Roasted Banana Coffee Cake

Roasting bananas is a simple way to use not-quite-ripe-enough-for-baking bananas without having to wait on Mother Nature to work her magic while they sit on the countertop. When I want to make banana bread, this coffee cake, or anything baked with bananas, I rarely have the patience for them to brown. 99.9% of the time I roast them in the oven to speed up the process. It only takes 15 minutes and is as simple as throwing a couple of bananas on a baking sheet and sliding them in the oven.

I love to make this coffee cake on special occasions like Mother's Day, Easter, or when I have a low-key brunch with friends. Don't let the word "cake" in the title mislead you; there's also the word "banana," which means it's suitable for breakfast. High-five.

SERVES 8 • TOTAL TIME: 65 MINUTES

DIRECTIONS:

- Preheat the oven to 350°F. Butter a 9-inch round cake pan with the 1 tablespoon room temperature butter and dust with the granulated sugar and tip out any excess.

- Place the bananas on a small rimmed baking sheet and roast for 15 minutes. Remove and set aside to cool.

- In a small bowl, combine the pecans, brown sugar, and cinnamon. Set aside.

- Sift the flour, baking soda, baking powder, and nutmeg through a fine-mesh strainer into a medium bowl.

- In the bowl of a stand mixer fitted with the paddle attachment, beat together the butter and sugar on low speed until light and fluffy, 2 to 3 minutes. Add the eggs one at a time, mixing well after each addition. Scrape down the sides of the bowl with a spatula, then add the roasted bananas, sour cream, and vanilla. Beat until incorporated.

INGREDIENTS:

8 tablespoons (1 stick) unsalted butter, melted and cooled, plus 1 tablespoon at room temperature for the pan

2 tablespoons granulated sugar

2 bananas

¾ cup chopped pecans

3 tablespoons dark brown sugar

1 teaspoon ground cinnamon

1½ cups unbleached all-purpose flour

1 teaspoon baking soda

1 teaspoon baking powder

¼ teaspoon freshly grated nutmeg

1 cup granulated sugar

2 large eggs, lightly beaten

¼ cup sour cream

1 teaspoon pure vanilla extract

- With the mixer running on low speed, spoon in the flour mixture and mix until just combined.

- Pour the batter into the prepared pan and smooth the top with a spatula. Sprinkle evenly with the pecan topping. Bake for 40 to 45 minutes, or until a toothpick inserted into the center comes out clean with a few crumbs attached.

- Let cool for 10 minutes before slicing and serving.

CHAPTER FOUR

Soups, Salads & Sandwiches

If I could conjure up the perfect meal, it would be a bowl of soup, a fresh, crisp salad, and some sort of sandwich. (Preferably a grilled cheese, but truthfully I'm not really picky.) Whenever I'm out to lunch, this is my go-to choice for the perfect meal trifecta, and more times than not I walk away blissfully satisfied.

It took me a while to feel comfortable making soup. I had always heard that soup is relatively easy, yet I was traumatized when I once tried to make a version of chicken noodle soup in a slow cooker. Well, that turned out to be an utter disaster, to say the least (think noodles swelling to an unnaturally huge size), so I gave up even attempting to make soup again for a year. Eventually, I got over that soup mishap. Now soup is something I make quite often, and with great success—but without the slow cooker, of course. I especially love soup in late summer or early fall when seasonal produce is in its prime, or in the winter on those days where I'm cold to the bone and a nice, hot bowl of soup is exactly what the doctor ordered.

I'm obsessed with salad, too: it's healthy, filling, and fresh, and the number of flavor combinations you can jam-pack into a bowl of salad is jaw-dropping. Salad doesn't have to be some plain old iceberg lettuce topped with a factory-made dressing. There's no reason to serve something so boring. I love to experiment with layering new textures, colors, and flavors—all critical steps to making the perfect salad.

Speaking of perfect, sandwiches are the very essence of an impeccable handheld meal: you can put pretty much anything between some sort of carb (or even lettuce) and it will be tasty. My favorite from this book? Well, let me just say that while I usually don't pick favorites, if I had to choose, it would be a tie between Herb-Crusted Shrimp Lettuce Wraps or the Grilled Adobo Turkey BBT Sandwich, which is a grilled cheese of sorts. So filling, so flavorful . . . and both contain bacon. Are you surprised I love them?

Feel free to let loose and have fun mixing, matching, and creating *your* perfect soup, salad, and sandwich combination. The different meals you can make using the recipes in this chapter are my idea of heaven—enjoy!

Soups, Salads & Sandwiches

Chipotle Butternut Squash Soup

Come fall, I'm itching to make anything and everything with butternut squash. I love it roasted and on top of a salad, or pureed with butter and spices, but at the tippy-top of my list is when it's in soup. In my honest opinion, butternut squash is best when it's blended velvety smooth—and it purees like a dream.

When I was thinking of what kind of butternut squash soup I wanted to put in this book, my mind immediately went to this simple spicy-meets-smoky recipe. This is a chipotle version made lusciously creamy with coconut milk and topped with a honeyed yogurt that lightly sweetens it and tempers the heat. While I love a creamy soup, I also love a little surprise of texture for balance. One day, an idea struck: I thought, *Why not toast those itty-bitty squash seeds in the oven with a little cumin and salt on top and throw them in?*

Genius move, I must say.

SERVES 4 TO 6 • TOTAL TIME: 45 MINUTES

DIRECTIONS:

- To make the soup: In a large Dutch oven, melt the butter over medium-low heat. Add the shallots and sauté for 5 minutes, until soft and translucent.

- Add the squash, chipotle and adobo, nutmeg, salt, and pepper. Raise the temperature to high and cook for 5 minutes more.

- Add the sherry and continue to cook until the sherry has reduced by half. Add the broth; if the broth doesn't cover the squash, add enough water to cover. Bring to a boil, then reduce the heat to low, cover, leaving the lid cracked, and simmer for 20 to 25 minutes, or until the squash is tender.

- Working in batches, use a ladle to carefully transfer the hot soup to a blender or food processor. Blend until smooth, then

INGREDIENTS:

FOR THE SOUP:

2 tablespoons unsalted butter

½ cup diced shallots

1 (3-pound) butternut squash, peeled and cut into 1-inch cubes

1 chipotle pepper in adobo, minced (about 1 tablespoon)

½ teaspoon adobo sauce

½ teaspoon freshly grated nutmeg

1 teaspoon kosher salt

½ teaspoon coarsely ground black pepper

¼ cup sherry

2 cups Vegetable Broth (page 46)

1 cup light coconut milk

FOR THE HONEYED YOGURT:

½ cup whole milk yogurt

1 tablespoon honey

FOR THE TOASTED SQUASH SEEDS:

Seeds from 1 butternut squash (about ½ cup)

½ teaspoon olive oil

½ teaspoon ground cumin

¼ teaspoon kosher salt

Chopped fresh cilantro, for serving

pour the soup back into the pot. (Alternatively, puree the soup directly in the pot with an immersion blender.) Add the coconut milk and keep warm over low heat.

- To make the honeyed yogurt: In a small bowl, whisk the yogurt and honey until smooth.

- To make the toasted squash seeds: Preheat the oven to 350°F. Rinse the seeds and pat dry. Place on a small baking sheet and toss with the olive oil, cumin, and salt. Spread the seeds in an even layer and toast in the oven for 8 to 10 minutes, or until crunchy. Watch them closely so they do not burn.

- Ladle the soup into bowls and serve with a dollop of honeyed yogurt, a sprinkle of fresh cilantro, and a few toasted squash seeds.

Bacon, Grilled Corn & Leek Chowder

The truth is that any recipe with the word "chowder" in it is more than all right in my book. Chowders are lusciously creamy, and as an added bonus, they can be eaten with those adorable oyster crackers. (If you have kids, they'll love that last bit.) This recipe just popped into my mind. What could be better than grilled corn, crispy bacon, and sautéed leeks in a big pot of chowder? And it doesn't disappoint. While testing it, I decided to make a little bacon-corn-chive topping to spoon on before serving, and I couldn't have been happier with the result. Fresh snipped chives really complete this chowder, and the bacon stays crispy. It's totally delicious.

SERVES 6 • TOTAL TIME: 45 MINUTES

DIRECTIONS:

- Heat a grill to medium. Brush the corn with olive oil and place on the grill grates. Grill for 10 to 12 minutes, turning the corn every so often. Once the kernels are bright yellow and tender, raise the grill heat to high and lightly char the outside. (Alternatively, cook the corn on a grill pan on the stovetop.) Transfer to a plate and let cool completely. Working with one corncob at a time, stand the corn in a bowl and cut downward to remove the kernels. Scrape the back of the knife over the cob to extract any extra juices directly into the bowl. Remove 1/3 cup of the corn kernels and set aside for garnish.

- While the corn is grilling, in a large Dutch oven, cook the bacon over medium heat until crispy, about 20 minutes. With a slotted spoon, transfer the bacon to a paper towel–lined plate and set aside to drain.

- Reduce the heat to medium-low and add the celery, carrots, and leeks to the bacon fat in the pot. Season the vegetables with 1 teaspoon of the salt and 1/2 teaspoon of the pepper. Sauté, stirring every so often, for 5 to 6 minutes, until softened.

INGREDIENTS:

4 medium to large ears sweet corn, husked

1 teaspoon olive oil or melted bacon fat

4 slices thick-cut applewood-smoked bacon, cut into 1/2-inch pieces

2 celery stalks, plus any leafy tops, diced (about 3/4 cup)

2 small carrots, diced (about 3/4 cup)

1 medium leek, quartered, rinsed, and patted dry

2 1/4 teaspoons kosher salt

3/4 teaspoon coarsely ground black pepper

1/4 cup unbleached all-purpose flour

4 cups Chicken Broth (page 45)

6 medium red-skinned potatoes, unpeeled, cut into 1/2-inch cubes

2 sprigs fresh thyme

1 bay leaf

1 cup heavy cream

2 tablespoons snipped fresh chives, for garnish

- Add the flour, stir, and cook for 1 to 2 minutes. Keep stirring while pouring in the broth, scraping up the brown bits on the bottom of the pot. Add the potatoes, thyme, and bay leaf. Cover, increase the heat to high, and bring to a boil. Reduce the heat to low, cover with the lid cracked a bit, and cook the potatoes for 15 minutes or until fork-tender.

- Add the cream, corn kernels, and any accumulated liquids in the bottom of the bowl and simmer the soup for 20 to 25 minutes more, or until thickened.

- Remove the thyme and bay leaf and stir. Taste and season with the remaining 1¼ teaspoons salt and ½ teaspoon pepper, or as desired.

- Just before serving, combine the reserved corn kernels, bacon pieces, and snipped chives in a small bowl. Ladle the soup into bowls and garnish with a spoonful of the corn, bacon, and chive mixture.

SIMPLY SCRATCH TIP

For extra texture, garnish with homemade Croutons (page 59).

Italian Sausage Pasta Fagioli

INGREDIENTS:

1 teaspoon olive oil

2 large links Italian sausage, casings removed, meat crumbled

1 medium yellow onion, chopped

3 cloves garlic, chopped

½ teaspoon Italian Seasoning (page 40)

½ teaspoon sugar

1 to 1½ teaspoons kosher salt

¼ teaspoon coarsely ground black pepper

6 cups Chicken Broth (page 45)

2½ cups cooked cannellini beans, or 2 (15-ounce) cans, drained and rinsed

2 (15-ounce) cans diced tomatoes

1 cup uncooked ditalini pasta

2 cups chopped fresh spinach leaves

¼ cup crumbled Parmesan cheese, for serving

Extra-virgin olive oil, for serving

This is one of those soups that you can make on a weeknight in just under an hour. Served with a crusty piece of Italian bread, it makes a complete meal—it's so delicious, hearty, and filling. Loaded with vegetables and beans, it's rustic and simple. The crumbles of Parmesan cheese and the drizzle of olive oil complete this one-pot masterpiece.

One pot. One soup. Do it.

SERVES 10 TO 12 • TOTAL TIME: 35 MINUTES

DIRECTIONS:

- In a large Dutch oven, heat 1 teaspoon of olive oil over medium heat. Add the crumbled Italian sausage and cook until browned, about 10 minutes. Transfer the sausage to a clean plate and set aside. Add the onion and garlic to the rendered fat in the pot and cook, stirring occasionally, for 3 to 5 minutes, or until soft. Add the Italian seasoning, sugar, salt, and pepper and cook for 1 minute.

- Return the sausage to the pot and add the broth, beans, tomatoes, and pasta. Cover and cook, stirring occasionally, until the pasta is cooked al dente, about 15 minutes.

- Add the spinach, cover, and cook until the spinach has wilted, 2 to 3 minutes.

- Ladle the soup into bowls. Sprinkle with some Parmesan cheese and drizzle with extra-virgin olive oil before serving.

SIMPLY SCRATCH TIP

I use either mild or hot Italian sausage for this soup. And when I'm feeling fancy, I'll go to the market around the corner and buy the house-made "rustic" sausage from the butcher. I'm not the biggest fan of sweet Italian sausage, but I bet it would work fine as well.

Creamy Roasted Tomato Soup

Let me just start by saying that I've never, *ever* liked tomato soup. For me, it always tasted too much like plain old tomato sauce. But everything changed when I came up with this recipe. It is so good that for the rest of eternity, I will LOVE tomato soup.

This creamy-yet-creamless soup has zero resemblance to the tomato soups that come from a can. When I first tried it, the flavors blew me away. I shared the recipe with my sisters to make sure I wasn't alone in enjoying its awesomeness. My sister Julie was the first to make it. She quickly snapped a picture and sent it to me in a text, confirming my thoughts: it's all kinds of amazing.

I like to top my bowl with homemade croutons and swirl in a spoonful of my homemade basil pesto. (I do this when I have some on hand in the fridge, because hello? Basil and tomatoes are practically BFFs.) Julie likes to top hers with crispy bacon. I support all of the above garnishes as possible toppings for this soup, and any ideas that you can dream up will be perfect, too—this soup is that versatile.

SERVES 6 • TOTAL TIME: 1 HOUR 10 MINUTES

DIRECTIONS:

- Preheat the oven to 375ºF.

- Place the tomatoes on a rimmed baking sheet, cut-side up, and drizzle with the olive oil. Season with 1 teaspoon of the salt and the oregano. Roast for 60 minutes, rotating the baking sheet halfway through.

- Meanwhile, in a large stockpot or Dutch oven, melt the butter over medium-low heat. Add the onion, carrots, and celery and season with the remaining 1 teaspoon salt. Cover and cook, stirring occasionally, for 20 to 25 minutes, or until the vegetables are tender. Once tender, add the garlic and cook for 1 to 2 minutes more.

INGREDIENTS:

12 medium to large plum (Roma) tomatoes, halved

2 tablespoons olive oil

2 teaspoons kosher salt

1½ teaspoons dried oregano

4 tablespoons unsalted butter

1 cup diced yellow onion (about 1 medium)

1 cup diced carrots (about 2)

1 cup diced celery (about 2 stalks)

4 cloves garlic, minced

2 cups Vegetable Broth (page 46)

2 tablespoons sherry

OPTIONAL GARNISHES:

6 tablespoons Basil Pesto (page 33)

Croutons (page 59)

Cracked black pepper

Crispy crumbled bacon

- Carefully transfer the sautéed veggies to a blender or the bowl of a food processor and add the broth, wine, and roasted tomatoes. Blend until smooth. Pour the pureed soup back into the pot and keep warm on low heat.

- Ladle the soup into bowls and serve with a dollop of pesto, crispy croutons, and cracked black pepper (and/or crispy bacon pieces!).

Southwest Chicken Chili

With ingredients like poblano and jalapeño peppers, and spices like ancho chile pepper and cumin, this chili doesn't lack in the flavor department. It's filling and comforting and unlike any other chili I've ever had in my life. This recipe originally appeared on my blog back in 2012, and because it's a favorite among readers and my family, I wanted to give it a mini make-over by simplifying it and lightening it up a bit for this book. This chili is perfect for a weeknight dinner or cozy Sunday at home—it's easy and delicious. The best part is that you can use leftover chicken from another meal in this recipe. In fact, you're encouraged to. Now how easy is that?

NOTE: If you'd like to use dried beans, see page 18 for soaking and cooking instructions.

SERVES 6 • TOTAL TIME: 45 MINUTES

DIRECTIONS:

- Place the chicken pieces in an even layer in a Dutch oven. Add the quartered onion, garlic, and bay leaf and add water to cover. Bring to a boil over high heat. Reduce the heat to medium-low, cover, and simmer for 14 minutes, or until the chicken is opaque and fully cooked. If you plan to reserve the cooking liquids for future use, skim off the foam that accumulates on the top of the water; otherwise, it's fine to leave it.

- Use tongs to transfer the chicken to a cutting board and let cool until safe to handle. Use two forks to shred the chicken.

- Wipe out the Dutch oven and melt the butter over medium heat. Add the diced onion, poblano, jalapeño, and garlic and sauté until tender, about 8 minutes.

- Season with the ancho chile powder, cumin, and 1 teaspoon of the salt. Sprinkle with the flour and stir until the flour is absorbed, then cook for 1 to 2 minutes.

INGREDIENTS:

2 pounds boneless, skinless chicken breasts and thighs

1 yellow onion, quartered, plus 2 cups diced yellow onion

2 cloves garlic, smashed and peeled

1 bay leaf

3 tablespoons unsalted butter

1 medium poblano pepper, seeded and diced (about ⅔ cup)

1 small jalapeño, seeds and ribs removed for less heat, if desired, and finely diced (about 2 tablespoons)

2 cloves garlic, minced

1 tablespoon plus 1 teaspoon ancho chile powder

2 teaspoons ground cumin

2¼ teaspoons kosher salt (more or less to taste)

3 tablespoons unbleached all-purpose flour

2 tablespoons tomato paste

3 cups Chicken Broth (page 45)

1 (15-ounce) can pinto beans, drained and rinsed

1 (15-ounce) can black beans, drained and rinsed

¾ cup frozen sweet corn kernels, thawed

Torn fresh cilantro leaves

Grated sharp cheddar cheese

Sour cream

Diced avocado

Tortilla chips

Cornbread (page 67)

- Stir in the tomato paste and cook for 1 minute. Add the chicken broth, beans, shredded chicken, and corn. Cover and simmer over low heat for 30 minutes. Taste and season with the remaining 1¼ teaspoons salt, or more or less to taste.

- Ladle the chili into bowls and serve topped with cilantro, cheddar cheese, a dollop of sour cream, diced avocado, and tortilla chips, or serve with a piece or two of cornbread.

SIMPLY SCRATCH TIP

To save yourself a step and a little time, you absolutely can use 3 to 4 cups of precooked shredded chicken in this chili.

Classic Greek Salad
with Pita Chip Croutons

INGREDIENTS:

2 Rustic Pita Bread (page 55), cut into 8 wedges each

1 tablespoon olive oil

¼ teaspoon kosher salt

Smoked paprika

10 ounces spring mix or your favorite salad greens

1 cup sliced English cucumbers (about 2 small)

1 cup quartered Campari tomatoes

½ small red onion, thinly sliced

½ cup crumbled feta cheese

½ cup Kalamata olives

1 recipe My Grandma's Greek Dressing (page 75)

Quartered cooked or pickled beets (optional)

Peperoncini peppers (optional)

½ cup cooked chickpeas (optional)

If you open my fridge, you'll always find the main ingredients for a hearty Greek salad. Sometimes I add things like pickled beets, chickpeas, and peperoncini, but I *always* have the bare bones of the salad on hand. I absolutely adore this Greek salad recipe. The feta, Kalamata olives, and Greek dressing create the key flavors and make an amazing combination.

For a heartier meal, I'd suggest making a double batch of My Grandma's Greek Dressing and using ¼ to ½ cup of it (it's okay to eyeball it!) as a 20-minute marinade for chicken breasts. In the summer, I'll cook the chicken on our outdoor grill, but in the cooler months I'll use my trusty cast-iron grill pan. When Greek salad is locked in my sight, there's no stopping me . . . not even the weather.

SERVES 4 TO 6 • TOTAL TIME: 30 MINUTES

DIRECTIONS:

- Preheat the oven to 400°F.

- On a rimmed baking sheet, toss the pita triangles in the olive oil. Season with the salt and sprinkle smoked paprika over the top. Spread them in an even layer and bake until toasted, 5 to 8 minutes.

- In a large bowl, combine the salad greens, cucumber, tomato, red onion, feta, and olives. If using, add the beets, peperoncini, and chickpeas. Drizzle with the dressing to taste right before serving with the toasted pita croutons.

Roasted Eggplant & Tomato Panzanella

Bread in salad: It's a beautiful thing. Panzanella is an Italian salad that features bread, tomatoes, and other ingredients mixed together. It's the perfect light dish, and it's especially delicious in the summertime, when tomatoes are fresh. The options are endless when it comes to the types of bread you can use, the array of vegetables to choose from, and the nuts and cheeses you can add. And there are tons of dressings that you can use in this panzanella that will work their way beautifully into the nooks and crannies of those crusty bread cubes.

Caprese anything is a huge hit in our house, so this is my version of my favorite caprese combination: roasted eggplant and tomatoes tossed with homemade croutons (cut a little larger than normal), as well as fresh mozzarella and torn basil leaves. I particularly love drizzling my Balsamic Herb Dressinade on this salad, but I encourage you to experiment! If you're looking for a salad that is totally out of this world, you've found it.

SERVES 6 TO 8 • TOTAL TIME: 25 MINUTES

DIRECTIONS:

- Preheat the oven to 400ºF.

- On a large rimmed baking sheet, toss together the tomatoes, 1 tablespoon of the oil, and ½ teaspoon of the salt. On a second rimmed baking sheet, toss together the eggplant, remaining 3 tablespoons olive oil, and remaining ½ teaspoon salt. Roast for 10 to 12 minutes. Let cool slightly, then transfer both vegetables and any juices to a large bowl.

- Add the croutons, mozzarella, basil, and dressinade. Toss together and season with pepper.

- Serve immediately at room temperature.

TIP: If you have a grill or one of those fancy grill pans, try grilling the tomatoes and eggplant.

INGREDIENTS:

2 pints cherry tomatoes

4 tablespoons olive oil

1 teaspoon kosher salt

1 medium eggplant, diced (about 4 cups)

6 cups (1-inch) Croutons (page 59)

1 cup fresh mozzarella balls

½ cup torn fresh basil leaves

¼ cup Balsamic Herb Dressinade (page 83)

½ teaspoon freshly ground black pepper

Lentil "Pasta" Salad

2 cups sprouted lentils

½ cup finely diced red onion

½ cup finely diced red bell pepper

½ cup finely diced orange bell pepper

½ cup finely diced yellow bell pepper

1 cup diced seeded unpeeled cucumber

1 cup halved cherry tomatoes (I like using both regular cherry and Sun Gold)

½ cup sliced black olives

¼ pound Genoa salami, cut into ½-inch cubes

1 recipe Italian Dressinade (page 84)

Kosher salt and coarsely ground black pepper

Over the summer, I had family over for a cookout to celebrate my daughter's thirteenth (gasp!) birthday, and a few of my family members are gluten- or dairy- and egg-free. I knew I wanted to make a salad that they could all enjoy with their burger, one that would cover all those bases.

I simply tossed cooked sprouted lentils, lots of freshly chopped veggies, and cubed salami with Italian Dressinade and an amazing pasta-less pasta salad was born.

This recipe totally happened on a whim. I never planned on it being in this chapter, or that it would actually taste as amazing as it did, and if it wasn't for my sisters going on about how they loved it . . . it may not have graced these pages. Whether or not you're gluten- or dairy- and egg-free, this salad is unbelievably colorful, refreshingly light, and so good for you. Not to mention majorly delicious.

NOTE: Sprouted lentils are lentils that have been through a soaking process where the legume literally sprouts! You can purchase sprouted lentils online or at a major grocery store. If you are unable to find sprouted lentils, you can use regular lentils in this recipe. Follow the package instructions for cooking.

SERVES 10 OR MORE • TOTAL TIME: 25 MINUTES PLUS 1 HOUR TO OVERNIGHT

DIRECTIONS:

· In a medium pot, bring 6 cups water to a boil. Add the lentils and cook for 5 minutes. Turn off the heat, cover with a lid, and let the lentils sit for 2 to 3 minutes, or until tender. Drain off any excess water and allow to cool before transferring to a large bowl.

· Add the onion, bell peppers, cucumber, tomato, olives, and salami to the bowl with the lentils. Add the desired amount of dressing and toss. Taste and season with salt and pepper. Chill for at least 1 hour or overnight before serving.

Grilled Romaine "Wedge" Salad

I'm not kidding when I say this recipe will change the way you view salads. This is a stick-to-your-ribs salad with a lot of flavor. To make it, you grill halved romaine "wedges" quickly, to give them a quick kiss of char, then top them with an herbed blue cheese dressing, crispy bacon, and sweet cherry tomatoes. Don't have a grill? Or maybe it's wintertime and there's a foot of snow outside? Not to worry. You can totally do this on a grill pan indoors.

When I was testing this whole grilled romaine concept, I asked my older daughter, Haileigh, to give it a try (she's my salad eater). I'll admit, she was a little skeptical at first, but after the first bite she was completely, 100 percent sold and claimed it was the best salad EVER. The incredible toppings don't hurt, either.

The problem-that-really-isn't-a-problem is that now I want all salads to have grilled romaine!

SERVES 4 • TOTAL TIME: 25 MINUTES

DIRECTIONS:

- In a large skillet, cook the bacon over medium heat until crispy. Transfer to a paper towel–lined plate to cool and drain, then coarsely chop.

- Meanwhile, heat your grill or a grill pan to medium-high.

- Remove any loose or wilted outer leaves from the halved romaine heads. Lightly brush the cut side of the romaine with olive oil. Place the halves cut-side down on the grill. Use another pan to weigh them down so they are pressed gently against the grill grates. Cook with the grill open for 2 to 3 minutes, or until grill marks appear. The romaine should not be wilted.

- Serve the grilled romaine with spoonfuls of dressing, halved tomatoes, crispy crumbled bacon, and a pinch of salt and pepper.

INGREDIENTS:

4 slices thick slab bacon (applewood, pecanwood, or peppered)

2 small to medium heads romaine, halved lengthwise with core intact

Olive oil

Herb Blue Cheese Dressing & Dip (page 71)

1 cup halved cherry tomatoes

Kosher salt and freshly ground black pepper

Ancho Chicken Chopped Salad with Zesty Catalina Dressing

I actually used to enjoy eating my salad plain. That's right—as in, no salad dressing. Zip, zilch, zero. And few vegetables besides lettuce. Who knows why? I don't. I swear, I had the strangest eating habits growing up, but now I'm all about colorful, tasty salads. I love to consider the rainbow when selecting the veggies and toppings that grace my greens. Red? Beets, tomatoes, Craisins. Green? Asparagus, cucumber, scallions. Yellow? Corn, chickpeas, squash. The more, the merrier. Nothing makes me want to eat a salad more than a beautiful bowl of greens that has a lot of great textures, colors, and flavors, and an awesome dressing drizzled over the top to boot. Because who wants to eat an ugly salad? Answer: NO ONE.

This salad is everything you could want: a vibrant array of vegetables, topped with tortilla chips and pepitas for crunch, grilled (and might I add, perfectly spiced) ancho chicken for flavor, and a zesty Catalina dressing to seal the deal. It's simple to put together, but you'll want to plan a little in advance—the dressing can be served immediately but tastes best if you refrigerate it for at least two hours, and the chicken is tastiest if it can marinate for a half hour.

SERVES 4 TO 6 • TOTAL TIME: ABOUT 60 MINUTES

DIRECTIONS:

- To make the dressing: In the bowl of a mini food processor, pulse the onion and garlic until finely chopped. Add the ketchup, 2 tablespoons of the vinegar, the honey, sugar, Worcestershire, salt, paprika, black pepper, and cayenne and process until smooth. Taste and add more vinegar, if desired. Pour into a glass jar or container with a tight-fitting lid and refrigerate for 2 hours or overnight.

INGREDIENTS:

FOR THE DRESSING:

1 small onion, quartered

2 cloves garlic

½ cup homemade Ketchup (page 29)

2 to 4 tablespoons red wine vinegar

¼ cup honey

¼ cup packed light brown sugar

1 tablespoon Worcestershire sauce

1 teaspoon kosher salt

1 teaspoon paprika

¾ teaspoon freshly ground black pepper

½ teaspoon cayenne pepper

FOR THE ANCHO CHICKEN:

2 cloves garlic

1 tablespoon ancho chile powder

½ teaspoon kosher salt

¼ teaspoon freshly ground black pepper

Juice of 1 lime (about 2 tablespoons)

1 tablespoon olive oil

1 pound boneless, skinless chicken breast halves (about 4)

⅓ cup fresh cilantro leaves

1 large head romaine lettuce, finely chopped

1 cup cherry tomato halves

1 small orange bell pepper, finely diced

1 cup fresh or frozen cooked sweet corn (thawed, if frozen)

2 avocados, finely diced

½ cup finely diced red onion

½ cup pepitas

Blue corn tortilla chips

- To make the chicken: Pass the garlic through a garlic press into a shallow bowl. Add the ancho chile powder, salt, pepper, lime juice, and olive oil. Whisk to combine.

- Place the chicken in the marinade and turn using tongs to coat all sides. Cover with plastic wrap and let the chicken marinate on the counter for 30 minutes.

- Lightly brush the grates of your grill with olive oil, then heat the grill to medium-high. Once it's hot, place the chicken on the grates and grill for 6 to 8 minutes per side, or until cooked through. Transfer the chicken to a platter, tent with aluminum foil, and let rest for 6 to 8 minutes.

- Chop the chicken into medium pieces. Sprinkle with fresh cilantro and continue chopping until the chicken is in small pieces.

- To assemble the salad: Divide chopped lettuce, chicken, tomato, bell pepper, corn, avocado, red onion, and pepitas among salad plates. Drizzle with the zesty Catalina dressing and serve with blue corn tortilla chips on the side.

Grilled Adobo Turkey BBT Sandwich

There's no denying my adoration for a good sandwich. And I think carefully about how a sandwich should be stacked. I always begin with really good bread and include a plethora of fillings that add color, texture, and, of course, flavor.

In this sandwich, you'll find turkey seasoned with olive oil and Adobo Seasoning, grilled, and then paired with crispy bacon, fresh basil, and tomato. But what knocks this sandwich out of the park is a schmear (or two) of romesco sauce and slices of a not-so-typical cheese, Manchego. All of which live happily ever after surrounded by grilled sourdough bread—until you eat this sandwich, of course.

MAKES 4 SANDWICHES • TOTAL TIME: 45 MINUTES

DIRECTIONS:

- Place the turkey in a large bowl or resealable bag. Add the oil and adobo seasoning, toss to coat, and set aside on the counter to marinate.

- In a large skillet, cook the bacon (in batches, if needed) until crispy, about 30 minutes.

- Heat a grill pan between medium and medium-high heat. Place the seasoned turkey on the pan and cook for 2 to 3 minutes per side, adjusting the heat so as to not burn, 12 to 14 minutes total. Transfer to a cutting board to rest for 5 minutes before slicing.

- Reduce the heat under the grill pan to medium or medium-low. Butter one side of each piece of bread. On one of the unbuttered sides, spread 1½ tablespoons of the romesco sauce. Place the bread, sauce-side up, on the grill pan and top with 2 slices of cheese, some basil, a few slices of tomato, bacon, sliced turkey, remaining cheese slice, and a second piece of

INGREDIENTS:

1 ¼ pounds turkey tenderloins

2 teaspoons olive oil

1 ½ tablespoons Adobo Seasoning (page 38)

9 slices thick slab bacon

4 tablespoons unsalted butter

8 slices sourdough bread

6 tablespoons Romesco Sauce (page 87), plus more for serving

12 thin slices Manchego cheese

16 fresh basil leaves

Thinly sliced tomato

buttered bread, sauce-side down. Grill for 3 to 4 minutes, or until grill marks form, then carefully flip and repeat.

- Cut in half and serve with more romesco sauce for dipping.

Herb-Crusted Shrimp Lettuce Wraps

I'm thinking these shrimp lettuce wraps should come with a warning label because when you eat them, you experience a major flavor explosion in every single bite. Consider yourself warned.

These delicious shrimp are coated in a mouthwatering combination of herbs, garlic, and red pepper flakes. And then cooked in bacon fat. Yup, you read that right. All that flavor goodness gets nestled in crisp, tender butter lettuce leaves and topped with bacon, sweet cherry tomatoes, and fresh corn. And if that doesn't have your taste buds aching, try topping them with my 5-Minute Avocado Spread. So, so good, you guys!

SERVES 4 TO 6 (MAKES 8 TO 10 WRAPS) • TOTAL TIME: 30 MINUTES

DIRECTIONS:

- In a 10-inch skillet, cook the bacon over medium heat until crispy. With a slotted spoon, transfer the bacon to a paper towel-lined plate. Drain off all but 1 tablespoon of the rendered bacon fat from the skillet.

- In a large bowl, combine the cilantro, parsley, chives, garlic, salt, black pepper, red pepper flakes, and olive oil. Add the shrimp and stir to combine.

- Heat the bacon fat in the skillet over medium-high heat. Working in batches, add the shrimp in a single layer and cook for 2 to 3 minutes before flipping and cooking for 2 to 3 minutes more, or until shrimp are cooked through. Use immediately, or transfer to an airtight container and refrigerate until ready to serve.

- Arrange 3 cooked shrimp per lettuce leaf and top with bacon, corn, tomatoes, and a small spoonful of the avocado spread. Garnish with a few snipped chives.

INGREDIENTS:

4 slices applewood-smoked slab bacon, halved lengthwise and cut into ½-inch pieces

2 tablespoons minced fresh cilantro leaves

2 tablespoons minced fresh parsley leaves

1 tablespoon snipped fresh chives, plus more for serving

2 cloves garlic, minced

½ teaspoon kosher salt

⅛ teaspoon freshly ground black pepper, plus more as needed

¼ teaspoon red pepper flakes

1 teaspoon olive oil

1 pound peeled and deveined shrimp (26 to 30)

8 to 10 butter lettuce leaves

1 cup fresh or frozen cooked sweet corn kernels (thawed if frozen)

1 cup halved grape tomatoes

1 recipe 5-Minute Avocado Spread (page 80)

SIMPLY SCRATCH TIP

In the summertime, skewer shrimp on metal or wooden skewers (soak wooden skewers in water for at least 1 hour before using) and grill!

Greek Lamb Pita Pockets

FOR THE CUCUMBER-DILL
YOGURT DRESSING:

1 cup plain Greek yogurt

½ cup finely diced unpeeled
English cucumber

2 tablespoons chopped fresh dill

1 clove garlic, minced

1 tablespoon fresh lemon juice

¾ tablespoon white wine vinegar

¾ teaspoon kosher salt

FOR THE LAMB PATTIES:

1½ pounds ground lamb

¼ cup crumbled feta cheese,
plus more for serving

2 cloves garlic, minced

1 tablespoon Greek yogurt

2 tablespoons minced fresh
cilantro

1 tablespoon minced fresh mint

1¼ teaspoons ground cumin

1 teaspoon kosher salt

¼ teaspoon cayenne pepper

TO ASSEMBLE:

4 Rustic Pita Bread (page 55),
cut in half for pockets

8 lettuce leaves, torn

1 small red onion, thinly sliced

1 tomato, thinly sliced

If you're looking for a sandwich with tons of flavor, then stop what you're doing because *this is it*.

In this recipe, you mix ground lamb with feta, fresh cilantro, mint, and spices . . . aka all the things I crave. Then you bake and stuff it into Rustic Pita Bread with crisp lettuce, red onion, and tomatoes. A few spoonfuls of the most amazing cucumber dill sauce ties everything together.

Translation: I love these.

SERVES 6 TO 8 • TOTAL TIME: 45 MINUTES

DIRECTIONS:

- To make the cucumber-dill yogurt dressing: In a small bowl, whisk together all the ingredients. Cover and refrigerate until chilled and ready to serve.

- To make the lamb patties: Preheat the oven to 400ºF. Line a baking sheet with parchment paper.

- In a large bowl, use a fork to combine all the ingredients; do not overmix. Measure 2 tablespoons of the lamb mixture and form into 2-inch oblong patties. Arrange the patties on the lined baking sheet and bake for 18 to 20 minutes. Transfer the cooked patties to a paper towel-lined plate before assembling the sandwiches.

- To assemble: Tuck 2 to 3 patties into each of the pita halves and fill with torn lettuce, red onion, sliced tomatoes, more feta (if desired), and some yogurt dressing.

SIMPLY SCRATCH TIP

Use a fork whenever you mix ingredients into meat so that you don't overmix the mixture and make dense, rubbery patties.

Ultimate Steak & Mushroom Sandwiches

INGREDIENTS:

1 ¼ to 1 ½ pounds rib-eye steak

1 cup Balsamic Herb Dressinade (page 83)

1 tablespoon unsalted butter

1 tablespoon olive oil

1 large sweet onion, halved and thinly sliced

1 pint cremini mushrooms, cleaned and sliced

Kosher salt and freshly ground black pepper (optional)

½ cup crumbled blue cheese

1 ½ cups grated provolone cheese

4 (6-inch) hoagie buns, split

Homemade Mayonnaise (page 25)

I try not to use words like "ultimate," "best," or "perfect" when it comes to recipe titles. But this sandwich is an exception. It's the ultimate because this sandwich combines my love for blue cheese, sautéed onions, and steak. Oh yeah, and there's crusty bread involved.

I often make my Easy French Bread (page 54) with this sandwich in mind. I slice the bread in half lengthwise, smear it with homemade mayo, divide the cooked meat and mushroom mixture over the top, sprinkle with cheese, and slide it under the broiler until the cheese has melted. For an out-of-this-world, open-faced sandwich that you need a knife and fork to eat, this is, quite honestly, one of the best things I've ever had.

MAKES 4 (6-INCH) SANDWICHES • TOTAL TIME: ABOUT 1 HOUR 30 MINUTES

DIRECTIONS:

- Place the steak on a small rimmed baking sheet and freeze for 20 minutes so it's firm and partially frozen. Holding a sharp knife on a slight angle, going against the grain of the meat, slice into very thin strips.

- In a large resealable bag or a medium bowl, marinate the steak in the Balsamic Herb Dressinade for 30 minutes.

- On a griddle or in a 12-inch cast-iron skillet, melt the butter with the olive oil over medium-high heat. Add the onion, toss, and spread out in an even layer. Once the onion starts to soften, add the mushrooms. Cook until soft and slightly caramelized.

- Using tongs, remove the steak from the marinade (allow excess marinade to drip back into the bowl or bag) and place on the griddle, toss with the onions and mushrooms, then spread in an even layer. Allow the steak to sear, forming a crust, for 4 to 6 minutes, then flip and cook for 4 to 6 minutes more.

- Season with a pinch of salt and pepper, if desired, and sprinkle with the blue cheese and provolone. Turn off the heat on the griddle or remove the skillet from the heat and cover with a domed lid or tented foil to allow the cheese to melt quickly.

- Toss one last time so the cheese is mixed throughout. Divide the steak mixture among the crusty hoagie buns. Serve immediately.

CHAPTER FIVE

Sides

I could write an entire book on side dishes. Side dishes are the pearl earrings to that little black dress, also known as the main dish. Delicious sides complete a meal and can turn something ordinary into something extraordinary. I mean, look at Thanksgiving. Sure, I love the turkey, but really it's more about the green bean casserole and those velvety mashed potatoes for me. Side dishes also allow you to explore tons of vibrant flavor combinations and keep your meals distinct and new. After all, nothing is more boring than eating the same things every week. When I'm looking for a nice, comfortable meal on a cold winter night, my sides will be hearty, loaded with filling, wholesome ingredients to keep my family warm. On a summer evening with friends, I like to serve sides with fresh vegetables simply dressed in a light sauce—and, of course, a glass of wine.

My point? Sides can dramatically transform your meal. Sides are your opportunity to shine.

Some of my favorites are roasted broccoli or cauliflower, or a simple salad. I don't want to make an even bigger mess in my kitchen if I don't have to, and I definitely don't want to spend several hours preparing every meal. But the real secret is that you don't have to spend a lot of time cooking a side dish for it to be delicious and the perfect match to your main dish.

In this chapter, you will find a little bit of everything: simple recipes that require minimal effort and use easy-to-find pantry ingredients; and recipes that are a smidgen more involved and intensive (but I promise, nothing that's too crazy!). You will even find a few dishes that could be meatless meals all on their own. And don't even get me started on side dish leftovers! Sides are usually even better the next day, and nine times out of ten you can slap an egg on them and serve them for breakfast, or toss them with a little cooked chicken and have a whole new meal for lunch or dinner. (Not dessert, though, because, um, hello? We all need chocolate for dessert, am I right?) Moral of the story is, serve me all the sides in the pages ahead—and give me a fork—and I'm a happy girl.

Sides

Oven-Roasted Butternut Squash with Brown Butter & Crispy Fried Sage

The title pretty much says it all. But to repeat: roasted butternut squash drizzled with browned butter and topped with crispy fried sage. I really have no words to describe how much I love this recipe.

One bite and I'm betting you'll know exactly why.

SERVES 6 TO 8 • TOTAL TIME: 45 MINUTES

DIRECTIONS:

- Preheat the oven to 400°F. Position one oven rack in the lowest position and one in the center.

- On a large rimmed baking sheet, toss the squash with the oil and salt. Roast for 30 minutes, or until fork-tender, rotating the baking sheet to ensure even browning. In the last 5 minutes of roasting, move the baking sheet to the middle of oven. Let cool for 5 minutes, then transfer the squash to a serving dish.

- Meanwhile, melt the butter in a small skillet over medium heat. Slowly cook the butter, stirring occasionally, until browned and fragrant. Turn off the heat, remove the skillet from the burner, and add the sage. Cook the sage leaves in the browned butter until crispy, 30 to 45 seconds. Use a slotted spoon to transfer the sage leaves to a paper towel–lined plate.

- Pour the browned butter over the roasted squash, sprinkle with the sea salt, and top with the crispy fried sage leaves.

- Serve warm.

INGREDIENTS:

1 (3-pound) butternut squash, peeled and cut into 1-inch cubes

1 tablespoon olive oil or sunflower oil

½ teaspoon kosher salt

4 tablespoons unsalted butter

10 to 15 fresh sage leaves, sliced

½ teaspoon flaky sea salt

Honey-Glazed Carrots

INGREDIENTS:

4 tablespoons unsalted butter

1 pound carrots, cut into roughly 1-inch chunks

½ teaspoon kosher salt

1 tablespoon minced garlic

½ teaspoon chopped fresh thyme leaves

1 tablespoon honey

1 tablespoon minced fresh flat-leaf parsley

SIMPLY SCRATCH TIP

I've discovered that not all honeys should be considered equal. I've bought cheap honey before because I was in a pinch, and it was horrible. Now I'm a firm believer that you get what you pay for. Good-quality honey should have less than 18 percent water content and be golden to dark in color. Using good-quality honey will definitely make a noticeable difference in any recipe, and it's not much more expensive.

If there's one dish that reminds me of my childhood, it's glazed carrots. I used to avoid cooked carrots like my life depended on it. Whenever we had meat loaf, I knew I could expect glazed carrots to be its sidekick, and I had to figure out a way to somehow eat or hide them. And eating them was out of the question. My mom called them "nature's candy." I used to think, *Puh-lease!* Hand me a carrot straight from the garden and I'd rinse it off with the hose and gladly eat it on the spot. But cooked carrots? Uh, no thanks.

I'm not sure how, when, or why I changed my mind about cooked carrots, but it eventually did happen. Maybe I just needed to grow up, or tell myself, "Uh, hello, Laurie! They're coated in honey *and* butter!" I mean, *seriously*. These glazed carrots are now easily one of my favorites: caramelized carrots, garlic, honey, and butter . . . and then there's the whole one-pan thing, too.

SERVES 4 • TOTAL TIME: 35 MINUTES

DIRECTIONS:

- In a 10-inch skillet, heat the butter and carrots over medium heat. Season with ¼ teaspoon of the salt and toss to coat once the butter has melted. Cook for 20 minutes, stirring occasionally, until the edges caramelize and the carrots are fork-tender.

- Decrease the heat to low and add the garlic, thyme, and honey. Stir and cook for 1 to 2 minutes, or until the honey butter glaze has thickened. Season with the remaining ¼ teaspoon salt, if desired.

- Sprinkle the glazed carrots with the parsley and serve immediately.

Parsnip Fries

I have an idea: the next time you're craving french fries, why not skip over the russets and snatch up a few parsnips? They only need around 10 minutes in a hot oven and are absolutely delicious.

I like to dip my parsnip fries in just about everything from Spicy Southwest Dip (page 70) to homemade Ketchup (page 29). And recently (thanks to my sister Kelly), I baked up a batch of these here fries, spooned leftover chili onto them, and topped it all with shredded cheddar cheese. So you see, not only is this a side dish, but you could easily turn it into a snack that's perfect for the Super Bowl, a night with friends, or just for a family treat. (Chili cheese parsnip fries . . . you must.)

SERVES 4 TO 6 • TOTAL TIME: 20 MINUTES

DIRECTIONS:

- Preheat the oven to 450°F.
- Cut the parsnips into 2½ by ½-inch sticks and toss them with the oil, salt, and paprika. Spread evenly onto two rimmed baking sheets and roast for 8 to 10 minutes, rotating the baking sheets halfway through cooking. Once golden brown, serve immediately.

INGREDIENTS:

2 large parsnips, peeled

2 tablespoons olive oil

¾ teaspoon flaky sea salt

1 teaspoon smoked paprika

Broccoli White Cheddar Gratin

I love broccoli. Like, really love it. Raw, roasted . . . *grilled* (amazing!). It's the one vegetable I literally crave all the time. And what better way to show some love to my favorite vegetable than to dress it with a white cheddar cheese sauce? I can think of none. Can you?

To make this side, start with a base of Cream of Chicken Soup, then add cream, freshly grated nutmeg, red pepper flakes, and Vermont white cheddar cheese, pour it all over the broccoli, then top with *more* cheese and bake. Simply perfection.

My daughter Haileigh gives this side dish a 9.5 out of 10. When I asked her what I could add to make it a 10, she said bacon. I like the way she thinks.

SERVES 4 TO 6 • TOTAL TIME: 55 MINUTES

DIRECTIONS:

- Preheat the oven to 350°F. Butter a 2-quart oval baking dish. Put the broccoli in the baking dish and set aside.

- In a small saucepan, combine the soup, cream, salt, black pepper, nutmeg, and red pepper flakes. Whisk until smooth, then cook over medium-low heat until the mixture thickens slightly. Stir in 1 cup of the cheese.

- Pour the cheese sauce over the broccoli in the baking dish and top evenly with the remaining 1/2 cup cheese.

- Bake for 30 to 35 minutes.

- Let cool for 5 minutes before serving.

INGREDIENTS:

½ tablespoon unsalted butter

1 recipe Cream of Chicken Soup (page 42)

½ cup heavy cream

¾ teaspoon kosher salt

⅛ teaspoon coarsely ground black pepper

⅛ teaspoon freshly grated nutmeg

Pinch of red pepper flakes

1½ cups grated Vermont white cheddar cheese

8 cups fresh broccoli florets (from about 4 heads)

Roasted Garlic Whipped Cauliflower

INGREDIENTS:

2 heads cauliflower, cut into florets

¼ cup bacon fat, melted

1 head roasted garlic (see page 17)

1 teaspoon kosher salt

¼ teaspoon coarsely ground black pepper

½ cup Vegetable Broth (page 46)

I fell completely in love with whipped cauliflower one night during a dinner at my sister Julie's house. Until then, I had no idea it even existed. It was so good, I had fourths. Four helpings of guilt-free goodness. So I figured that since I could hardly tell the difference between whipped cauliflower and mashed potatoes, I'd try to pull a fast one on my family. Yup, I tried to trick my family into thinking they were mashed potatoes. And my girls totally fell for it. . . . Pat knew something was up, though, because they were so velvety smooth, and my mashed potatoes are never so fluffy. I was totally busted. (He still ate 'em, though!)

This whipped cauliflower has roasted garlic mixed with bacon fat all whipped together into a creamy bliss.

MAKES 4 CUPS • TOTAL TIME: 30 MINUTES

DIRECTIONS:

- Preheat the oven to 450ºF.

- On a large rimmed baking sheet, toss the cauliflower with the bacon fat and roast for 20 to 25 minutes, or until caramelized.

- Squeeze the cloves from the head of roasted garlic and transfer to a blender. Add the roasted cauliflower, salt, pepper, and broth. Blend until smooth.

- Serve immediately or keep warm in a medium saucepan over low heat until ready to serve.

SIMPLY SCRATCH TIP

Roasting garlic takes about 45 minutes, but sometimes I do a bunch of garlic at once to have on hand. Roasted garlic lasts for about 2 weeks in the fridge or up to 3 months in the freezer.

Roasted Beets with
Parsley Pesto Vinaigrette

Beets are so nutritious, and the girl in me loves their gorgeous jewel-tone colors. Roasting beets is my favorite method to prepare them: it requires no dirtying of pans, just a few pieces of aluminum foil that can later be pitched.

For this recipe, I toss the still-warm beets in a ridiculously easy parsley pesto vinaigrette and sprinkle with chopped pistachios and flaky sea salt for a stunning, light side dish that's wholesome, insanely flavorful, and definitely unique.

SERVES 6 • TOTAL TIME: 1 HOUR 15 MINUTES

DIRECTIONS:

- Preheat the oven to 425ºF.

- Divide the beets among two sheets of heavy-duty aluminum foil. If you are using different-colored beets, keep them separated. Seal the edges of the foil to create packets and place directly on the oven rack. Roast for 45 minutes to 1 hour. Let cool until safe to handle.

- While the beets are roasting, whisk together the pesto and vinegar and set aside.

- Peel the beets under cool running water with your hands or use a kitchen towel, gently rubbing each beet to remove their skins, then quarter.

- In a serving bowl, gently toss the beets with the vinaigrette. Sprinkle with the pistachios and sea salt before serving.

INGREDIENTS:

1½ pounds medium beets (8 to 10), trimmed and scrubbed well

¼ cup Parsley Pesto (page 35)

2 tablespoons red wine vinegar

3 tablespoons coarsely chopped pistachios

Flaky sea salt

Adobo Green Beans with Toasted Garlicky Almonds

My younger daughter, Malloree, has a hard time liking green vegetables. You know: asparagus, broccoli, green beans, and any salad that calls for lettuce. She has come a long way over time (thanks to her fabulous mother's cooking). She'll now eat a salad that is drenched in ranch dressing—but hey, I'll take it. So you can totally imagine my shock when I witnessed her shoveling these green beans into her mouth. Her reason: "These are actually really good, Mom." Thanks, Malloree.

I now make these at least twice a month. They are the perfect side dish to my Turkey and Vegetable Meat Loaf (page 223), Blackberry-Glazed Salmon (page 245), or alone in a bowl when it's just you and a night of catching up with your DVR.

Not that I've ever done that.

SERVES 6 TO 8 • TOTAL TIME: 30 MINUTES

DIRECTIONS:

- Bring a large pot of water to a boil and add a heavy pinch of salt.

- Heat 1 tablespoon of the oil in a 12-inch cast-iron skillet over medium-low heat. Add the garlic and slowly cook for 1 to 2 minutes until softened and golden brown. Add the chopped almonds and cook, stirring occasionally, for 4 to 5 minutes, or until toasted and fragrant. Remove the skillet from the heat, transfer the nuts to the small dish. Set aside.

- Add the green beans to the boiling water and cook for 5 to 6 minutes. Drain in a colander and immediately rinse with cold water. With a kitchen towel, pat the beans completely dry.

- Meanwhile, wipe out the skillet and heat the remaining 1 tablespoon olive oil over medium-high heat. Add the beans

INGREDIENTS:

½ teaspoon kosher salt, plus a heavy pinch

2 tablespoons olive oil

3 tablespoons minced garlic

⅓ cup finely chopped almonds

1 pound fresh green beans, trimmed

1½ teaspoons Adobo Seasoning (page 38)

¼ teaspoon paprika

and toss to coat. Season with the adobo seasoning, paprika, and remaining 1/2 teaspoon salt and toss. Cook, stirring occasionally, for 8 to 10 minutes, or until the beans start to brown. They should be tender but still have bite to them.

· Serve on a platter topped with the garlicky almonds.

Sour Cream & Chive Smashed Potatoes

This side dish couldn't be any easier: seven simple ingredients and one pot is all you need.

In the spring and summer months I have a huge chive plant that I make good use of. So believe me when I tell you I make these ALL THE TIME. I always serve them with our family favorite Home-Style Baked Chicken (page 209). No potato peeling required, lumps are encouraged, and fresh chives are a must.

NOTE: Baby red potatoes are my favorite potato to use in this recipe, but small Yukon Gold or even russets can be substituted. Just cut the russets into 1¹⁄₂-inch pieces before boiling.

SERVES 8 • TOTAL TIME: 35 MINUTES

DIRECTIONS:

- Place the potatoes in a large pot and add cold water to cover the potatoes by 1 inch. Bring the water to a boil and cook the potatoes until fork-tender, 10 to 15 minutes.

- Drain the potatoes and return them to the pot over low heat. Add the butter and use a potato masher to smash until the potatoes are lumpy.

- Switch to a large spatula and add the sour cream, milk, salt, pepper, and chives. Keep covered and warmed over low heat until ready to serve.

SIMPLY SCRATCH TIP

Can't find fresh chives? Use the dark green parts of 4 scallions.

INGREDIENTS:

3 pounds unpeeled baby red or baby Yukon Gold potatoes, scrubbed

6 tablespoons (¾ stick) unsalted butter

½ cup sour cream

⅓ cup whole milk

1 ½ teaspoons kosher salt

½ teaspoon coarsely ground black pepper

3 tablespoons snipped fresh chives

Twice-Baked Sweet Potatoes

I'm ever so diligently trying to convert my family into sweet potato aficionados. It's a work in progress, but recipe by recipe, meal by meal, I hope they're starting to see that sweet potatoes are just as good as (if not better than) regular potatoes.

I, on the other hand, am irrevocably in love with them. I love them mashed with jalapeños. I love them simply diced and roasted, or made into breakfast home fries. But twice-baked? Those are my jam. This recipe is perfectly spiced with chili powder and cinnamon and sweetened with maple syrup, and, of course, butter is involved. Who even needs a main dish when there are twice-baked potatoes? I'm not kidding.

SERVES 4 • TOTAL TIME: 1 HOUR 30 MINUTES

DIRECTIONS:

- Preheat the oven to 400°F.

- Massage the olive oil onto the sweet potatoes and set them on a small baking sheet. Bake for 1 hour or until a knife glides through effortlessly. Let cool until safe to handle. Keep the oven on.

- Halve the sweet potatoes horizontally and carefully scoop out the flesh into a medium bowl. Set the skins aside. Add the butter, maple syrup, chili powder, cinnamon, and ¼ teaspoon of the salt and use a potato masher to mash the filling until smooth.

- In a small bowl, combine the honey, pecans, and a pinch of salt.

- Place the skins side by side in a small baking dish. Spoon the filling in, dividing it evenly, and top with with the honeyed pecans. Bake for 5 minutes.

- Serve warm.

INGREDIENTS:

2 medium sweet potatoes, scrubbed

1 teaspoon olive oil

4 tablespoons unsalted butter

2 tablespoons pure maple syrup

2 teaspoons chili powder

½ teaspoon ground cinnamon

½ teaspoon kosher salt, plus a pinch

2 tablespoons honey

¾ cup coarsely chopped pecans

Farro Fried "Rice"

1½ cups farro, rinsed and drained

½ teaspoon kosher salt

¼ pound (4 slices) applewood-smoked bacon, cut into ½-inch pieces

½ cup diced red onion

½ cup finely diced carrot

½ cup diced cubanelle pepper

1 clove garlic, minced

1 large egg, beaten

⅓ cup thawed frozen peas

I'm forever on the hunt for different sides to serve with dinner besides the recurring roasted broccoli. Although I love it so, I just can't serve it every night (mainly because my family would revolt). Whenever I'm out to dinner, I'm always scoping out the menu for inspiration. I once had something similar to this recipe at a restaurant and was instantly intrigued. Not familiar with farro? It's a delicious hulled wheat grain that's similar to barley. Farro has a nutty flavor and cooks similarly to rice; I've even made farro risotto, or farrotto, before.

In this faux fried rice dish, farro meets bacon and a hodge-podge of vegetables. Miraculously, you can make it in one pan *and* have it ready in 30 minutes. Prepare to fall madly in love.

SERVES 6 • TOTAL TIME: 30 MINUTES

DIRECTIONS:

- In a large pot with a tight-fitting lid, combine the farro, ¼ teaspoon of the salt, and 4 cups water. Bring to a boil, reduce the heat to medium-low, cover, and cook for 15 minutes. Drain off any extra water, rinse, and set off to the side.

- In a wok or 12-inch skillet, slowly heat the bacon over medium heat to render out the fat. Once the bacon is crispy, use a slotted spoon to transfer it to a plate. Drain off all but 1 tablespoon of the bacon fat in the pan. (Discard the remaining bacon fat or transfer to a jar, let cool, and store in the fridge for a later purpose.)

- Add the onion, carrot, and cubanelle to the pan with the bacon fat, stir, and cook for 5 to 8 minutes, or until softened. Add the garlic and cook for 1 minute. Add the farro and return the bacon to the skillet. While stirring, slowly pour in the egg until cooked. Add the peas and remaining ¼ teaspoon salt, toss, and cook until heated through.

- Serve warm.

Corn & Jalapeño Sauté

I love, love, *love* a simple side dish, and nine times out of ten that is the only kind I will make on a weeknight. Who has time for a side dish that takes *hours*? I save those kinds of recipes for the weekend. Maybe.

This sauté is so incredibly easy and so darn good. I love to serve it as a bed underneath Broiled Chili-Lime-Crusted Tilapia (page 249) or next to grilled chicken, or keep a meal vegetarian by eating it by itself. It keeps well in the fridge, which makes for excellent leftovers for lunch.

SERVES 4 TO 6 • TOTAL TIME: 35 MINUTES

DIRECTIONS:

- Melt the butter in a large skillet over medium heat. Add the jalapeños and sauté until tender, about 8 minutes. Add the garlic and cook for 1 minute. Add the corn, bell pepper, and tomatillos and cook for 4 to 5 minutes.

- Season with the chili powder, cumin, salt, and black pepper. Stir in the scallions and chopped cilantro. Keep warm over low heat until ready to serve.

INGREDIENTS:

2 tablespoons unsalted butter

2 small jalapeños, seeded and diced

4 cloves garlic, minced

2½ cups fresh or frozen sweet corn kernels (thawed, if frozen)

½ cup diced red bell pepper

1 cup diced tomatillos

½ teaspoon chili powder

½ teaspoon ground cumin

½ teaspoon kosher salt

¼ teaspoon coarsely ground black pepper

6 scallions, sliced

2 tablespoons chopped fresh cilantro

Garlicky Creamed Spinach

INGREDIENTS:

4 tablespoons unsalted butter

1 medium shallot, minced

3 cloves garlic, thinly sliced

¼ cup unbleached all-purpose flour

2 cups whole milk

½ teaspoon kosher salt

⅛ teaspoon freshly grated nutmeg

1 bunch fresh spinach (about 10 ounces), stems removed and discarded, leaves chopped

⅓ cup grated Parmesan cheese

This lusciously creamy spinach is SO good, I've been known to eat a bowl of it simply by itself. I've even spread it on garlic toast before. In my husband's words, "It's pretty darn amazing," and he's not a huge fan of spinach, to say the least. I've often considered throwing a few quartered artichoke hearts into this heavenly side dish for a spinach-artichoke version. Yup, that will definitely be happening.

This is another one-pan side dish that quickly comes together in 30 minutes. Saddle it up next to baked chicken, pork chops, or grilled (and buttered) crusty slices of bread.

And don't flake out and skip the nutmeg. It truly makes the dish.

SERVES 6 • TOTAL TIME: 30 MINUTES

DIRECTIONS:

- In a deep 12-inch skillet or Dutch oven, melt the butter over medium-low heat. Add the shallots and garlic and sauté until soft, about 5 minutes. While whisking, gradually add the flour and cook for 2 to 3 minutes. Continue to whisk while slowly pouring in the milk. Season with salt and nutmeg. Add the chopped spinach, using tongs to toss and coat in the sauce. Cover the pan and cook, stirring occasionally, until the spinach wilts into the sauce.

- Add the Parmesan, stir, and serve immediately.

Baked Beans

A version of these baked beans originally debuted on my blog in 2012. It's my mom's recipe, and even though they taste absolutely incredible, they are far less "from scratch" than what you would expect. I've always sort of had it in the back of my mind that I wanted to figure out a way to make a more from-scratch version of the beloved baked beans from my childhood. Now I've done it.

These baked beans take only minutes to prep, and the rest is taken care of in the oven. The intoxicating mixture of bacon, onions, molasses, and spices like ground cloves will have your mouth watering before you even take a bite. Promise.

SERVES 10 • TOTAL TIME: 4 HOURS

DIRECTIONS:

- Follow the cooking tips for soaking and cooking dried beans on page 18. If you are using canned beans, you can skip this step.

- Preheat the oven to 350ºF.

- Combine the bacon and onion in a medium Dutch oven. Slowly cook over medium heat until the onion is tender and the bacon is cooked, 8 to 10 minutes.

- Meanwhile, in a medium bowl, whisk together the ketchup, molasses, sugar, ground mustard, ground cloves, and 1 cup water to combine. Add the cooked beans and pour the mixture into the pot with the bacon and onion. Stir, cover, and bake for 1 hour, stirring every 20 minutes.

- Add the salt and stir. Uncover and let sit for 15 to 20 minutes before serving.

INGREDIENTS:

1½ cups dry navy beans, or 2 (15-ounce) cans navy beans, drained and rinsed

4 slices applewood- or pecan wood–smoked bacon, cut into 1-inch pieces

1 cup diced yellow onion

1½ cups Ketchup (page 29)

¼ cup plus 2 tablespoons unsulphured molasses

½ cup packed dark brown sugar

1¼ teaspoons ground mustard

1 teaspoon ground cloves

1 teaspoon kosher salt

Smashed Cast-Iron-Skillet Potatoes with Chimichurri

INGREDIENTS:

8 medium red potatoes

2 teaspoons olive oil

Kosher salt and freshly ground black pepper

½ cup Chimichurri Sauce (page 88)

Cotija cheese

All right, so picture this: you toss a few red potatoes in some olive oil, tip them into a screaming-hot cast-iron pan, and roast them until the skins are crisp and a fork effortlessly glides through. THEN you bust them up with a potato masher, season with some S & P, spoon chimichurri sauce over, and top each one with a sprinkle of Cotija cheese.

Sounds amazing, right? You can also make this recipe with smaller, "new" potatoes. Just follow the same steps (though expect that they'll need less time in the oven) and serve them as an appetizer.

These potatoes are so filled to the brim with flavor that you won't even miss the butter and sour cream.

SERVES 4 TO 6 • TOTAL TIME: 55 MINUTES

DIRECTIONS:

- Place a 12-inch cast-iron skillet in the oven and preheat the oven to 400ºF.

- Wash the potatoes and dry them well. In a large bowl, toss the potatoes with the olive oil. Using potholders, slide the oven rack out and place the potatoes in an even layer in the hot pan. Bake the potatoes for 50 to 60 minutes, or until fork-tender.

- Remove the skillet from the oven and let the potatoes cool slightly, about 5 minutes. Use a potato masher to gently press on the potatoes until they burst. Season with a few pinches of kosher salt and pepper before topping with a few spoonfuls of chimichurri and sprinkling with Cotija. Serve warm.

Wild Rice & Orzo Pilaf with Dried Cherries & Almonds

When I was young, my sister Julie and I absolutely hated rice pilaf. Or maybe it was just that I went along with Julie because I was the youngest of four girls and was easily persuaded. Yeah, that has to be it. As I've shared with you many times, my mom is an excellent cook, but there were a few things my little self just could not accept, things like pistachio pudding, TVP (textured vegetable protein), and my mom's Italian beef pie (sorry, Mom!). And, of course, there was the rice pilaf. I'm still not a fan of the pudding (that will NEVER happen) and the TVP, but rice pilaf is definitely something I've grown to love!

I make my pilaf by pan-toasting orzo pasta with butter, shallots, and garlic, then mixing in rice and baking it in the oven with fun add-ins like dried cherries and almonds. It is so simple and yet so, SO good!

MAKES 8 CUPS • TOTAL TIME: 1 HOUR 25 MINUTES

INGREDIENTS:

2 tablespoons unsalted butter

1 medium shallot, diced

2 cloves garlic, minced

¾ cup orzo pasta

¾ cup long-grain white rice

¼ cup wild rice blend

¾ cup chopped dried cherries

¾ teaspoon kosher salt

4 cups Vegetable Broth (page 46)

⅓ cup sliced almonds

⅓ cup sliced scallions

DIRECTIONS:

- Preheat the oven to 375°F.

- Melt the butter in a 10-inch skillet over medium-low heat. Add the shallot and cook until soft, 4 to 5 minutes. Add garlic and cook for 1 to 2 minutes more. Increase the heat to medium-high, add the orzo, and toast for 5 to 6 minutes, stirring occasionally.

- Transfer the toasted orzo, white and wild rice, cherries, and salt to a 2-quart baking dish (that has a lid). Pour half of the broth over the rice and stir. Cover and bake for 45 minutes. Remove the lid, add the remaining broth, and bake for 40 minutes more, or until the wild rice is tender. Note that wild rice tends to have a more textural bite to it.

- Transfer to a serving dish and toss with the sliced almonds and scallions before serving.

Bacon Braised Greens

4 slices applewood-smoked bacon, cut into ½-inch pieces

1 cup thinly sliced red onion

2 cloves garlic, smashed and peeled

1 teaspoon dried oregano, crushed in your palm

1 teaspoon kosher salt, plus more as needed

¼ teaspoon red pepper flakes

1 large plum (Roma) tomato, seeded and diced

1 bunch kale, stems removed and leaves coarsely chopped (about 8 cups)

1 bunch collard greens, stems removed and leaves coarsely chopped (about 8 cups)

1¾ cups Chicken Broth (page 45)

2 teaspoons apple cider vinegar

¼ teaspoon coarsely ground black pepper

These braised greens are an absolute must at any family summertime barbecue. Vitamin-rich, dark leafy greens braised in bacon fat? I mean, seriously.

IMPORTANT TIP: I'd suggest serving the greens and all that glorious broth in a separate small bowl. It's really a personal preference because I like to drink the bacon-y broth after I eat the greens. (If this doesn't sound appetizing, try it before you knock it—you'll love it.) But serving this dish separately means the broth won't mess up your Baked Beans (page 183), or make the bun of your grilled brat soggy. Is there a worse cookout tragedy than that? No.

These greens aren't strictly summer fare, either. They can be made any day of the year. Try them with Cornbread & Leek Stuffed Pork Chops (page 228) as well!

SERVES 8 TO 10 • TOTAL TIME: 40 MINUTES

DIRECTIONS:

- In a large Dutch oven, cook the bacon over medium heat until browned, about 8 minutes. Add the onion, garlic, oregano, salt, red pepper flakes, and tomato. Stir and cook until the onion is tender, 5 to 6 minutes.

- Stir in the kale, collard greens, and broth. Cover and cook the greens until wilted, stirring occasionally, 15 to 20 minutes. Stir in the vinegar and season with salt and black pepper before serving.

Buttermilk Cream Corn

INGREDIENTS:

4 to 6 ears corn

2 tablespoons unsalted butter

2 cloves garlic, minced

¾ teaspoon kosher salt

¼ teaspoon coarsely ground black pepper

1½ cups heavy cream

½ cup buttermilk

⅓ cup sliced scallions (dark parts only)

¼ teaspoon red pepper flakes

Fresh corn is a total must when making creamed corn because underneath the kernels is where the liquid gold is. It's that "corn milk" that gives this side dish a natural and subtle sweetness, and you just cannot get it from using thawed frozen corn or canned corn. It takes a few minutes to prep the corn, and beware: you might even graffiti your walls with some of the milk when you scrape the cobs. But don't let that deter you, because this dish is honestly stand-in-the-middle-of-the-kitchen-scarfing-down-an-entire-bowl kind of good. The slight tang from the buttermilk, the sweetness from the corn, and the sharp, bright scallions combined with a little heat from the red pepper flakes truly make for a side made in creamed corn heaven.

SERVES 4 TO 6 • TOTAL TIME: 35 MINUTES

DIRECTIONS:

- With a sharp knife, cut the kernels off the corncob and place them in a large bowl. With the back of the knife, scrape the corn milk out of the cob and into the bowl with the kernels.

- In a 10-inch skillet, melt the butter over medium heat. Add the garlic and cook for 1 to 2 minutes. Then add the corn kernels and corn milk into the skillet and season with the salt and pepper. Cook over medium heat for 3 to 4 minutes. Reduce the heat to medium-low and add the heavy cream.

- Simmer until the mixture has reduced by half, 12 to 15 minutes. Turn off the heat and stir in the buttermilk. Scoop two ladles (about 1 cup) of the corn mixture into a blender or food processor and puree until smooth. Add the pureed corn back to the pan along with the scallions and red pepper flakes; do not reboil. Stir and serve warm.

Dijon Roasted Brussels Sprouts

These sprouts were something I served completely by accident. One night, I needed a quick side to go with pork tenderloin and mashed potatoes, and I opened the fridge looking for inspiration. I had a bunch of Brussels sprouts that desperately needed to be used up, and my eyes darted to the country-style Dijon mustard in my fridge door. Gears started turning in my head, and I went over and raided my spice drawer. Thus this recipe was born.

I got a thumbs-up all around—yes, even the ever-so-picky green-vegetable-hater Malloree approves of this dish—so naturally I've been making these ever since.

SERVES 4 TO 6 • TOTAL TIME: 35 MINUTES

DIRECTIONS:

- Preheat the oven to 400°F.

- Place the halved Brussels sprouts onto a rimmed baking sheet.

- In a small bowl, whisk together the oil, mustard, paprika, garlic powder, and onion powder and pour the mixture over the sprouts. Using your hands, toss to coat and arrange the Brussels sprouts cut-side down on the baking sheet. Season with the salt right before sliding into the oven and roast for 20 to 30 minutes, or until fork-tender. Remove, season with the pepper, and serve immediately.

INGREDIENTS:

1½ pounds fresh Brussels sprouts, trimmed and halved

2 tablespoons olive oil or sunflower oil

1 tablespoon country-style Dijon mustard

½ teaspoon smoked paprika

⅛ teaspoon garlic powder

⅛ teaspoon onion powder

½ teaspoon kosher salt

¼ teaspoon freshly ground black pepper

SIMPLY SCRATCH TIP

Cooking times will vary depending on the size of the Brussels sprouts. When picking your sprouts at the grocery store, if they're loose, try to pick ones that are equal in size so they'll cook uniformly.

Blistered Brown Sugar & Sesame Sugar Snap Peas

Crank your oven to 500°F, toss the ingredients in this recipe onto a baking sheet, and slide it into the oven. Easy-peasy. I usually just eyeball the measurements because: no bowls + no spoons = no dishes to wash. Just how I like it.

SERVES 4 TO 6 • TOTAL TIME: 15 MINUTES

DIRECTIONS:

- Preheat the oven to 500°F.

- On a rimmed baking sheet, toss together the snap peas, oil, and sugar and spread the peas out evenly. Roast for 8 to 10 minutes.

- Toss with the sesame seeds and season with the sea salt. Serve immediately.

INGREDIENTS:

1 pound sugar snap peas

1½ teaspoons toasted sesame oil

1 tablespoon dark brown sugar

2 teaspoons black sesame seeds, for garnish

½ teaspoon flaky sea salt

Skillet Refried Black Beans

So easy. So good. After you taste these beans, you won't even consider buying canned refried beans ever again. I've made these 4,782 times (and counting), and it's safe to say my family absolutely loves them. While we're waiting on the rest of dinner to finish cooking, you can find us hovering over the skillet, armed with tortilla chips and putting a major dent in them as if they were a dip. We also smear a spoonful of these beans onto tortillas before adding the makings for fajitas, and use them in nachos. The flavor is out of this world, and if for some reason you aren't too crazy about black beans, you can always substitute pinto beans instead.

SERVES 4 TO 6 • TOTAL TIME: 15 MINUTES

DIRECTIONS:

- In a large cast-iron skillet, heat the lard over medium-low heat. Add the onion and sauté for 5 minutes, or until soft and translucent. Stir in the garlic, chili powder, cumin, and coriander and cook for 1 to 2 minutes. Add the beans and the broth (water may be substituted in a pinch). Using a potato masher, smash the beans until they are the desired consistency. You can add more broth if they are too thick. Bring to a simmer over medium-high heat and stir in the cilantro. Cook for 2 to 3 minutes, until the beans have thickened. Add the grated cheese and stir until melted. Garnish with more cilantro and serve immediately.

INGREDIENTS:

2 tablespoons lard or bacon fat

1 cup diced white onion

1 clove garlic, minced

1 teaspoon chili powder

½ teaspoon ground cumin

½ teaspoon ground coriander

2 cups cooked black beans, or 2 (15-ounce) cans black beans, drained and rinsed

½ cup Vegetable or Chicken Broth (pages 46 and 45), plus more as needed

2 tablespoons minced fresh cilantro, plus more for serving

1 cup freshly grated pepper jack or Monterey Jack cheese

1 teaspoon kosher salt

SIMPLY SCRATCH TIP

Feel free to change it up and use pinto beans—everything else stays the same and they're equally delicious.

Fajita Vegetable Stir-Fry

It took me many, many years to warm up to cooked bell peppers. Really, *all* cooked vegetables, but peppers took the longest for me to get over my initial heave-inducing reflex. Growing up, I'd fork through my bowl of chili to spot and get rid of them, or pick them off of pizza. I might've even removed the piece of cheese the pepper was touching on the pizza, too. I know. DRAMA! Even though I still can't imagine myself ever eating and actually enjoying a dish like stuffed peppers where the peppers are the star, I do love quite a few recipes that use them as an ingredient . . . especially this stir-fry.

I'm not fooling you when I say that this stir-fry is *easy*! It's also extremely versatile, which I love. Some days I serve it with Broiled Chili-Lime-Crusted Tilapia (page 249), or use it to fill our chicken fajitas. It's also perfect for a meatless quesadilla, or tucked into a breakfast burrito or omelet. Seriously, the sky is the limit.

NOTE: It's never a bad idea to have your *mise en place* ready for this recipe, whether you prep the vegetables the night before and stick them in a container so they're ready to use or prep them right before stir-frying. This is a fast-paced side dish, so having everything ready to go will save you time.

SERVES 4 TO 6 • TOTAL TIME: 20 MINUTES

DIRECTIONS:

- In a large wok or 12-inch cast-iron skillet, melt the butter with the olive oil over high heat.

- Once the pan is screaming hot, add the onion and ½ teaspoon of the salt. Toss the onion to coat in the butter and olive oil and leave undisturbed for 2 minutes to develop a char. Stir once and let cook for 2 minutes more. Once the onion is charred yet still a bit firm, add the bell and poblano peppers. Cook for 4 minutes, stirring occasionally.

INGREDIENTS:

1 tablespoon unsalted butter

1 tablespoon olive oil

1 large sweet onion, halved and sliced

½ teaspoon kosher salt

1 red bell pepper, seeded and sliced

1 orange bell pepper, seeded and sliced

1 poblano pepper, seeded and sliced

1 cup fresh or frozen sweet corn kernels (thawed if frozen)

4 cloves garlic, minced

1 jalapeño, seeded, if less heat is desired, and sliced

2 tablespoons chopped fresh cilantro

Juice of ½ lime

Kosher salt

- Add the corn, garlic, and jalapeño and cook, stirring often, for 2 to 3 minutes more, until the corn is heated through.

- Add the cilantro and lime juice. Taste and season with more salt if desired. Serve immediately.

Cheesy Polenta

Creamy, cheesy polenta is a major weakness of mine. I don't mind scalding the taste buds off my tongue by eating it straight out of the pot. I'm not sure what it is, but it has comfort—aka cheese!—in every bite. I tend to serve ridiculous amounts of cheesy polenta with braised anything, and I never regret it.

This polenta is also perfect in my Vegetarian Polenta Skillet (page 101). Just omit the cheese and dice it after it has cooled and add to the skillet. Or, like I said, eat it soft straight out of the pot.

SERVES 4 • TOTAL TIME: 10 MINUTES

DIRECTIONS:

- Measure the corn grits and add the salt to the measuring cup.

- In a medium saucepan, bring the milk and broth to a boil. Watch carefully, because it will start to boil quickly. Whisk in the corn grits and salt; keep whisking until the corn grits have absorbed all the liquid. Add the cheese and pepper. Stir until smooth and serve immediately.

INGREDIENTS:

1 cup coarse yellow corn grits (or polenta)

¾ teaspoon kosher salt

2 cups whole milk

1 cup Chicken Broth (page 45)

1 cup grated Vermont cheddar cheese

¼ teaspoon coarsely ground black pepper

Grilled Scallions with Dijon Vinaigrette

INGREDIENTS:

2 bunches scallions

1 tablespoon olive oil

¼ teaspoon kosher salt

⅛ teaspoon coarsely ground black pepper

¼ cup Warm Dijon Vinaigrette (page 73)

I was first introduced to the idea of eating whole scallions by my husband and his parents. They put a little salt in the bottom of a glass, trim off the rooty tips of the scallions, and simply dip them into the salt and eat them. As crazy as it sounded when I first tried it, it's actually a really tasty way to eat them. It got me looking at scallions differently, and made me realize they don't just have to be a garnish.

And since I've tried grilling just about anything and everything—including grapes (done it) and pound cake (did it)—it was only a matter of time before I'd come up with grilled scallions. Grilling them takes away some of their sharp bite, and the char will only enhance their amazingness. Pour a little warm (or cool works, too) Dijon vinaigrette on top, and it's the perfect side dish for a grilled main. Try them next to the Grilled Rib-Eye Steaks with Mushroom-Shallot Butter (page 238). Beyond delicious. Perfect for those summer nights spent on the patio, and mighty pretty on a plate, too.

SERVES 4 TO 6 • TOTAL TIME: 20 MINUTES

DIRECTIONS:

- Heat a grill with a medium to medium-high flame. If you are using a grill pan, heat over medium to medium-high heat.

- On a rimmed baking sheet, toss the scallions with the olive oil, salt, and pepper.

- Place the scallions on the grill grates and grill for 3 to 4 minutes before turning them. Then grill for 2 to 3 minutes more on the other side.

- Transfer the scallions to a platter and drizzle with the warm Dijon vinaigrette. Serve immediately.

Curried Cauliflower with Golden Raisins & Pistachios

Not only is this curried cauliflower stunningly delicious, it's extremely light and healthy. The earthy spices mixed with the sweet raisins and crunch of pistachios make for an amazing and colorful side dish.

If I'm lucky enough to have leftovers afterward, I usually reheat this for my lunch the next day.

SERVES 4 • TOTAL TIME: 35 MINUTES

DIRECTIONS:

- Preheat the oven to 400ºF.

- In a large bowl, combine the cauliflower, oil, curry, turmeric, and sumac. Spread evenly onto a rimmed baking sheet and roast for 25 to 30 minutes until caramelized and tender.

- Season with salt and pepper and toss with the golden raisins, pistachios, and parsley before serving.

INGREDIENTS:

1 head cauliflower, cut into florets

¼ cup olive oil

1 tablespoon curry powder

½ teaspoon ground turmeric

¼ teaspoon ground sumac

½ teaspoon kosher salt

¼ teaspoon coarsely ground black pepper

⅓ cup golden raisins

¼ cup coarsely chopped pistachios

1 tablespoon minced fresh flat-leaf parsley

CHAPTER SIX

Mains

I think most people would agree that answering the "What's for dinner?" question can sometimes be cringe inducing. I'll actually brace myself, white-knuckling the countertop or steering wheel (depending), waiting for my family's reaction when I tell them what we're having, especially when *I know* it's something they'll be less than ecstatic about. Most days, it's all fist-bumps and happy dances, but sometimes I have to break it to them that "yes, there are mushrooms in the meat loaf," and "yes, you will be eating it." It's the role we play as parents, no? It also can be the role we play as spouses. . . .

Sometimes a freshly home-cooked meal isn't always in the cards, because let's face the music . . . life is crazy busy. There are days I feel like I'm circling around town picking up one kid and then dropping off the other between Haileigh's and Malloree's after-school sports. Throw in an evening dentist or haircut appointment for kicks, and dinnertime can sometimes be pushed back to seven or even eight p.m. On those days, I make an effort to prepare dinner earlier in the day and keep it in the fridge to reheat later.

I will say that no matter what's going on that day, or that week even, we always end up together at the dinner table. It has been important to me since my girls were little. Like so many families, the dinner table is where we recap the day, plan for the weekend, and air the nitty-gritty school drama. It's a slice of family time that's special, keeps us close and us parents in the know (so important!).

In this chapter, I wanted to share some of my favorite dinner mains: fresh takes on classics, new (and sometimes) spicy takes on others. There are quick recipes that are perfect for weeknights, like Broiled Chili-Lime-Crusted Tilapia (page 249), or my husband's favorite: Orange-Ginger Chicken & Rice (page 215). You will also find recipes that are just the ticket for a cozy weekend or weekday meal, if you're lucky to have a day off work. Dishes like Home-Style Baked Chicken (page 209), Turkey Vegetable Meat Loaf (page 223), or Spaghetti & Meatballs (page 235) are the types of easy meals that make my family's dinners so special. I've also included a few fancier recipes for those special occasion dinners (or if you just feel like having fun!). All are relatively simple to make and will knock you over with flavor. And, as a bonus: at the bottom of each recipe, you will find that I've suggested a side dish or two (or three!) from this book to pair with that main dish. So it helps you take the guesswork out of the whole "What's for dinner?" Boom. Meal planned.

Mains

Home-Style Baked Chicken

I'll be real with you: the best part of this baked chicken is the crispy spice-crusted skin. I may or may not be known for peeling off the skin of any chicken remaining on someone's plate (not always my own . . .), folding it, and eating it like a sandwich. It may sound strange, but I think you'll understand once you experience the heavenly deliciousness that is this skin.

This chicken recipe is a pick-up-with-your fingers-and-devour sort of situation. The juices drip down the sides of your hands, but you won't mind—or at least I don't—because your eyes will be closed as you enjoy the moist, tender, and juicy mouthful of chicken. Don't *even* bother to use a fork and knife. We don't.

SERVES 4 TO 6 • TOTAL TIME: 1 HOUR 20 MINUTES

DIRECTIONS:

- Preheat the oven and a 9 by 13-inch metal roasting pan to 375ºF. Place the olive oil and butter in the pan and place the pan in the oven on the lower rack.

- In a small bowl, combine the poultry seasoning, salt, and pepper. Set aside.

- Place the flour in a resealable bag. Place a few pieces of the chicken in the flour at a time, seal, and shake to coat. Remove and vigorously shake off any excess flour. Place the flour-dusted chicken on a clean platter. Repeat with the remaining chicken pieces.

- Remove the roasting pan from the oven and immediately arrange the chicken skin side up in a single layer over the bottom of the pan and then sprinkle with some of the poultry seasoning blend and paprika. It should sizzle.

- Place the hot pan back on the lower rack of the oven and bake for 20 minutes. Remove, baste by spooning the juices that have collected in the pan over each piece, and then sprinkle the chicken with the remaining poultry seasoning blend.

INGREDIENTS:

2 tablespoons olive oil

2 tablespoons unsalted butter

1 ½ teaspoons Poultry Seasoning (page 39)

1 teaspoon salt

¼ teaspoon freshly ground black pepper

1 cup unbleached all-purpose flour

½ teaspoon paprika

4 to 5 pounds skin-on, bone-in chicken thighs and drumsticks

- Return the pan to the oven and bake for 20 minutes more. Remove and baste one last time before moving the chicken to the middle rack and baking for 10 to 15 minutes more to further crisp the chicken skin.

- Let rest for 5 to 8 minutes before serving.

MAKE IT A MEAL

Sour Cream & Chive Smashed Potatoes (page 173), Buttermilk Cream Corn (page 190), or Roasted Garlic Whipped Cauliflower (page 166)

Lemon, Garlic & Herb Roasted Chicken

1 (3- to 4-pound) whole chicken

Kosher salt and freshly ground black pepper

1 head garlic

1 medium lemon

8 sprigs fresh parsley

4 sprigs fresh rosemary

3 sprigs fresh thyme

1 recipe Lemon, Garlic & Herb Compound Butter (page 86), at room temperature

2 tablespoons unbleached all-purpose flour

1 to 2 cups Chicken Broth (page 45)

It's true what they say: roasting a whole chicken is easier than it sounds. But I've never been nervous about the roasting—just the *trussing*. My mom has perfected the art of trussing, using one string to wrap, tuck, and tie turkey or chicken in one neat little bow. I bet she could do it blindfolded in her sleep (she's seriously that good at it). I did *not* inherit the trussing gene, so I simply do not tie the wings and legs with kitchen string. It doesn't look as fancy (sorry, Mom!) but the chicken tastes the same: delicious.

I typically make roasted chicken on Saturday or Sunday when I have a few hours to prep, roast, and make gravy (because I'm all about the gravy). I like to buy the two-pack of organic chickens from Costco and cook both at once, using the second bird for lunches and dinners throughout the week (especially for something like Southwest Chicken Chili, page 133). The leftover chicken is also great in soups or salads.

Your home will be engulfed in the aromas of a home-cooked meal, and whether you truss with the best of 'em or not, this lemony, garlicky, herb-roasted chicken is simple, moist, and so extremely flavorful. You'll never make another kind of roast chicken—I promise.

SERVES 2 TO 4 • TOTAL TIME: 2 HOURS

DIRECTIONS:

- Preheat the oven to 400°F.

- Pat the chicken dry with a paper towel.

- Season the inside of the chicken cavity with a couple pinches of salt and pepper.

- Slice off the top third from the head of garlic and cut the lemon in half. Tie the parsley, 3 sprigs of rosemary, and 2 sprigs of fresh thyme together with kitchen string and place the bundle inside the cavity along with the garlic head and lemon halves.

- Divide the compound butter in half. Starting at the neck, gently insert your fingers underneath the skin, working your way around and separating the skin from the chicken. Insert half the butter under the skin and rub it over the entire chicken. Take the remaining butter and slather it on the outside of the chicken, over the skin. Next, season the outside with ½ tablespoon of salt. Place the chicken on a rack set inside a cast-iron skillet or small roasting pan.

- Roast the chicken on the lower rack of the oven for 60 to 65 minutes, or until fully cooked. A thermometer inserted in the thickest part of the chicken should read 165°F and the legs should be loose and the juices clear. Baste the chicken with any pan juices and transfer to carving board, tent with aluminum foil, and let the chicken rest for 15 to 20 minutes.

- Remove the lemon, garlic, and herbs from the cavity before carving. Start by removing the wings, then the legs, and then remove the entire breast from the breastbone and slice.

- Pour all the pan drippings from the roasting pan into a glass measuring cup or fat separator. Once the juices settle and the fat rises, skim 2 tablespoons of the fat and return it to the roasting pan. Skim the remaining fat off the top and discard; this should leave about 1 cup (more or less) of juices behind. Pour in enough chicken broth to equal 2 cups total liquid.

- Set the roasting pan on the stovetop over medium heat. Sprinkle the flour into the pan. Whisk, cooking the flour for 2 to 3 minutes before slowly pouring the juices and broth into the pan.

- Add the remaining 1 sprig rosemary and 1 sprig thyme. Let the gravy bubble while you whisk until it thickens. Season with salt and pepper. Discard the herb sprigs before serving.

- Serve the sliced roasted chicken with a spoonful or two of gravy over the top.

MAKE IT A MEAL

Try it with Curried Cauliflower with Golden Raisins & Pistachios (page 203), Wild Rice & Orzo Pilaf with Dried Cherries and Almonds (page 187), Honey-Glazed Carrots (page 160), or Broccoli White Cheddar Gratin (page 165).

Orange-Ginger Chicken & Rice

When I first made this recipe, I served it to my family and watched with one eye closed as they all took their first bite. I was betting that there would be some haters because the suggestion of anything stir-fry in my house usually is followed by "There are way too many vegetables!" or "Are there peanuts in it?" But to my surprise, I was dead wrong.

My husband, the pickiest of them all, turned to me and said, "I taste orange and ginger." Then he said, "I *really* LIKE it." That was way more than I could have ever expected. I was flabbergasted.

I was hoping for the fresh-squeezed orange juice and ginger to shine through, but not be all-up-in-your-face annoying—know what I mean? There's a little heat from Sriracha in here, but you can customize that to your preference.

Dinner in 30 minutes? Sign. Me. Up.

SERVES 4 TO 6 • TOTAL TIME: 30 MINUTES

DIRECTIONS:

- In a large glass measuring cup, combine the garlic, ginger, orange zest, orange juice, sugar, tamari, Sriracha, and white pepper. Whisk until the sugar has dissolved.

- In a large bowl, toss the chicken with the salt, black pepper, and cornstarch.

- In a 12-inch skillet or wok, heat 1 tablespoon of the coconut oil over medium-high. Place half the chicken in the pan in an even layer and cook for 3 minutes before turning. Cook on the second side for 2 to 3 minutes more. Transfer to a clean plate and repeat with the remaining 1 tablespoon coconut oil and the rest of the chicken.

- Reduce the heat to medium. Return all the chicken to the pan, pour in the orange-ginger sauce, stir, and cook the

INGREDIENTS

6 cloves garlic, minced

¼ cup minced peeled fresh ginger

1 teaspoon orange zest

1½ cups strained fresh orange juice (from 3 to 4 large oranges)

2 tablespoons light brown sugar

2 tablespoons low-sodium tamari

½ to 1 teaspoon Sriracha

¼ teaspoon freshly ground white pepper

1½ pounds boneless, skinless chicken breasts, cut into bite-size pieces

½ teaspoon kosher salt

¼ teaspoon freshly ground black pepper

2 tablespoons cornstarch

2 tablespoons coconut oil

1 Cornstarch Slurry recipe (page 14)

3 cups cooked jasmine rice

Sliced scallions, for garnish

chicken for 4 to 5 minutes. Pour in the cornstarch slurry, stir, and cook until the sauce thickens.

- Serve over cooked jasmine rice and top with sliced scallions.

White pepper may not be the most common ingredient, but it adds a special and distinct pepper flavor to this sauce. I use it instead of black pepper in most of my stir-fry recipes.

MAKE IT A MEAL

Serve with Blistered Brown Sugar & Sesame Sugar Snap Peas (page 193), roasted broccoli, or sautéed bok choy.

Roasted Red Pepper, Sun-Dried Tomato & Feta Topped Chicken

This chicken dish was a decade in the making. It was inspired by a different, not-quite-from-scratch recipe I found in a magazine *years* ago. It was my go-to recipe when having girlfriends over for dinner because it is simple but looks oh-so-fancy.

Over the years I obliterated the original recipe, changing this and adding that, to make it more from-scratch. Instead of using bottled dressing for the chicken marinade, I now use My Grandma's Greek Dressing. I also roast my own red bell peppers, which, by the way, is better than what you find in the jars, in my opinion. Of course, jarred peppers will work just fine in a pinch! I also added capers for that distinct salty-briny taste. But if capers aren't your thing, try adding 1/2 cup small, quartered artichoke hearts, or 1/4 cup chopped Kalamata olives.

This recipe is forgiving—it's perfect for those of you who are newer to cooking—and it's adaptable to whatever pleases your palate.

SERVES 4 • TOTAL TIME: 40 MINUTES

INGREDIENTS:

DIRECTIONS:

4 boneless, skinless chicken breasts (6 to 8 ounces each)

1/2 cup My Grandma's Greek Dressing (page 75)

1/3 cup diced charred red bell pepper (see page 14)

1 tablespoon minced sun-dried tomatoes

1 tablespoon brined capers, rinsed and drained

1 tablespoon minced fresh flat-leaf parsley

1/4 teaspoon kosher salt

1/8 teaspoon freshly ground black pepper

3/4 cup crumbled feta cheese

1 tablespoon unsalted butter

1 tablespoon olive oil

- Preheat the oven to 350°F.

- Place the chicken in a medium bowl or large resealable bag and pour the Greek dressing over the top. Marinate the chicken on the countertop for 20 minutes. (Any longer and the lemon juice will start to break down or "cook" the chicken.)

- In a medium bowl, combine the bell pepper, tomatoes, capers, parsley, salt, black pepper, and feta.

- In a 12-inch cast-iron or other oven-safe skillet, melt the butter with the olive oil over medium-high heat. Remove the chicken from the marinade and let any excess marinade drip back into the bag. Place the chicken top-side down in the skillet and sear for 4 to 6 minutes. Turn the chicken over and divide the pepper and feta mixture over the top. Slide the skillet into the oven. Bake for 15 to 18 minutes, or until the chicken is cooked through. Carefully transfer the chicken to a platter and let it rest for 5 to 6 minutes before serving.

MAKE IT A MEAL

Adobo Green Beans with Toasted Garlicky Almonds (page 171) or Garlicky Creamed Spinach (page 180)

Creamy Chicken & Rolled Dumplings

This is classic comfort food and one of my family's favorite meals. It's a creamy, souplike stew, with carrots, celery, shredded chicken, and adorable little dumplings that are rolled and cut by hand.

It doesn't get any better than a bowl of this.

SERVES 6 TO 8 • TOTAL TIME: 1 HOUR 45 MINUTES

DIRECTIONS:

- To make the chicken: In a large stockpot, combine the celery, carrot, onion, parsley, bay leaf, and peppercorns. Place the chicken pieces over the vegetables and add 10 cups cold water or enough so the chicken is fully submerged.

- Bring the water to a boil; cover the pot, leaving the lid cracked; reduce the temperature to low; and simmer for 1 hour.

- Use tongs to remove the cooked chicken and transfer it to a cutting board to cool. Line a fine-mesh strainer with cheesecloth and set it over a large bowl. Strain the broth through the strainer; reserve the poaching liquid and discard the solids. Set aside 8 cups poaching liquid for this recipe; reserve any extra for another use or discard.

- Shred the chicken when cool enough to handle. Set aside 5 cups for this recipe; reserve any extra chicken for another use.

- To make the dumplings: In a large bowl, whisk together the flour and baking powder. Use a pastry cutter to blend the lard into the flour mixture. With a wooden spoon or rubber spatula, stir in the milk until a dough forms. On a lightly floured surface, roll the dough out to 1/8 inch thick. Use a sharp knife, pizza cutter, or ravioli cutter to trim the dough to make a 14 by 10-inch rectangle and then cut it into 3/4-inch squares.

- To assemble: In a large Dutch oven, melt the butter over

FOR THE CHICKEN:

1 celery stalk, coarsely chopped

1 carrot, unpeeled, coarsely chopped

1 medium yellow onion, coarsely chopped

4 sprigs fresh flat-leaf parsley

1 bay leaf

8 whole black peppercorns

1 (5-pound) cut-up chicken

FOR THE DUMPLINGS:

2 cups unbleached all-purpose flour

1 tablespoon baking powder

1/3 cup lard

3/4 cup whole milk

FOR THE STEW:

4 tablespoons unsalted butter

3/4 cup chopped yellow onion

2 celery stalks, sliced

2 carrots, unpeeled, sliced

2 1/2 teaspoons kosher salt, plus more as needed

2 cloves garlic, minced

1 1/2 teaspoons Poultry Seasoning (page 39)

1/4 cup unbleached all-purpose flour

1 cup whole milk

1 tablespoon minced fresh flat-leaf parsley, plus more for garnish

Cracked black pepper

To reheat any leftovers, simply place them in a saucepan and reheat slowly over medium-low heat until hot and bubbling.

medium-low heat. Add the onion, celery, and carrots and season with 1/2 teaspoon salt. Cook until softened.

- Add the garlic and cook for 1 to 2 minutes. Whisk in the poultry seasoning and the flour and cook for 2 to 3 minutes. While whisking, pour in the reserved 8 cups poaching liquid and the milk, increase the heat to medium, and bring to a gentle boil.

- Drop in the dumplings, one at a time, using a slotted spoon to press them down. Cook the dumplings for 8 to 10 minutes. Add the reserved 5 cups shredded chicken and the parsley and season with the remaining 2 teaspoons salt, or to taste. Reduce the heat to low and cook until the chicken mixture has thickened. Season with more salt, if desired.

- Ladle the chicken and dumplings into bowls and garnish with more minced parsley and black pepper.

MAKE IT A MEAL

This recipe is pretty satisfying all on its own, but it can be served with Adobo Green Beans with Toasted Garlicky Almonds (page 171), Dijon Roasted Brussels Sprouts (page 191), or a light, crisp salad. There's no such thing as too many veggies!

Turkey Vegetable Meat Loaf

Turkey meat loaf has never tasted so good. There's a sentence I'd never thought I'd ever say. But it's true! This meat loaf is filled with wholesome goodness like sautéed carrots, onions, and celery. Even mushrooms! Even my kids don't complain about mushrooms in this dish, or not now, anyway. . . .

When I first made this and served it to my family I: 1) didn't tell them there were mushrooms in it, and 2) also failed to mention it was turkey. No one realized until their plates were cleaned and I knew it was safe to spill the beans.

When something tastes this good . . . how could they be mad? Did I mention they cleaned their plates?!

SERVES 6 TO 8 • TOTAL TIME: 1 HOUR 25 MINUTES

DIRECTIONS:

- Preheat the oven to 375°F. Line a metal baking sheet with heavy-duty aluminum foil and lightly grease with olive oil. Set aside.

- Place the butter in a 12-inch skillet and melt over medium-low heat. Add the onion, carrot, and celery. Cover the pan and sauté, stirring occasionally, for 18 to 20 minutes, or until the vegetables are tender. Add the garlic and cook for 1 minute. Add the mushrooms, sage, and thyme. Stir and cook until the mushrooms are soft, 3 to 4 minutes. Transfer the vegetable mixture to a bowl to cool slightly.

- Meanwhile, in a large bowl, combine the turkey, bread crumbs, 1/4 cup of the ketchup, the Worcestershire, egg, salt, and pepper. Add the cooked vegetables and use a fork to combine the ingredients, then mix by hand just until combined (do not overmix). Transfer the meat mixture to the prepared baking sheet and form it into a loaf.

- Combine the remaining 1/3 cup ketchup and the brown sugar and stir until the sugar has dissolved. Set aside.

INGREDIENTS:

2 tablespoons unsalted butter

3/4 cup finely diced yellow onion

3/4 cup finely diced carrot (about 1 medium)

3/4 cup finely diced celery (about 1 stalk)

2 cloves garlic, minced

1 1/2 cups minced cremini mushrooms

3/4 teaspoon ground sage

1/2 teaspoon dried thyme

2 pounds ground turkey (85/15 fat ratio)

1 cup plain bread crumbs (see page 58)

1/4 cup plus 1/3 cup Ketchup (page 29)

1/4 cup Worcestershire sauce

1 extra-large egg, lightly beaten

3/4 teaspoon kosher salt

1/4 teaspoon coarsely ground black pepper

1 tablespoon packed dark brown sugar

- Bake the meat loaf for 20 minutes, then remove and brush with half the glaze. Bake for 20 minutes more, then remove, brush with the remaining glaze, and bake for 10 minutes more.

- Tent the meat loaf with foil and let rest for 5 to 8 minutes before slicing and serving.

MAKE IT A MEAL

Honey-Glazed Carrots (page 160), Adobo Green Beans with Toasted Garlicky Almonds (page 171), Sour Cream & Chive Smashed Potatoes (page 173)

Italian Sausage & Four Cheese Manicotti

INGREDIENTS:

Olive oil

14 manicotti shells (8 ounces)

Fine sea salt

3 hot Italian sausages (about 12 ounces), casings removed

2 cups Classic Marinara (page 78)

10 fresh basil leaves, rolled and thinly sliced

2 cups whole milk ricotta cheese

½ cup plus 2 tablespoons finely grated Parmesan cheese

2½ ounces (or ½ cup) sharp provolone cheese (diced into ½-inch cubes)

2½ ounces (or ½ cup) Fontina cheese (diced into ½-inch cubes)

1 tablespoon finely minced fresh flat-leaf parsley

The first time I ever made manicotti, I swore I'd never do it again. I came home at seven thirty after a very long twelve-hour shift, picked up my girls from my mother-in-law's, and then spent the next TWO hours stuffing shells and making a colossal mess of my entire kitchen as I went. I vowed that if I ever made them again—which I doubted I would—I would never wait until seven thirty p.m. with two starving kids under the age of six waiting with pleading eyes for dinner. But as important, I'd have to figure out a new way to stuff shells, one that didn't require me to make a faux-pastry bag from a resealable baggie. Those never work well for me, though I don't know why!

Oh, and I also realized I should have had an open bottle of wine on standby. Wine makes every dreadful task a little bit more fun.

I've fine-tuned a manicotti recipe to make it more doable. It will take you exactly one hour to prep and stuff fourteen manicottis, and that includes making the marinara on the spot! I know this because I'm a dork and literally timed myself. That said, this is definitely a multitasking recipe, so don't make it if you're in a rush. Once you pull off stuffing the shells and sprinkle them with Parmesan, it only takes another thirty minutes in the oven to make this amazing cheesy-sausage-stuffed masterpiece. Totally worth it all. I promise!

SERVES 6 TO 8 • TOTAL TIME: 1 HOUR 30 MINUTES

DIRECTIONS:

- Preheat the oven to 350ºF. Grease an 11 by 7-inch glass baking dish with 1 teaspoon of olive oil.

- Bring a large pot of water to a boil. Season with 1 tablespoon of sea salt and add the pasta. Cook for 2 to 3 minutes less than the package directions indicate, stirring occasionally. In the meantime, grease a baking sheet with ½ teaspoon of olive oil. Use tongs to transfer the shells from the water to the baking sheet. Let cool until they are safe to handle.

- Meanwhile, in a 12-inch skillet, crumble the sausage and cook over medium heat until browned, about 20 minutes. Use a slotted spoon to transfer the sausage to a paper towel–lined plate, leaving a little of the rendered fat in the pan.

- Reduce the heat to low, pour in the marinara, add the fresh basil, and heat until just warm. Pour ¾ cup of the sauce into the bottom of the greased baking dish.

- In a large bowl, combine the ricotta, ¼ cup of the grated Parmesan, the provolone, Fontina, parsley, and browned sausage. Use a teaspoon to stuff each of the shells. Arrange the stuffed shells in the prepared pan, cover with 1¼ cups of the marinara, and sprinkle with the remaining 6 tablespoons of grated Parmesan.

- Bake, uncovered, for 30 minutes or until browned and bubbling. Let cool for 5 minutes before serving.

MAKE IT A MEAL

Because this dish is more involved, I always serve it with a simple green salad and garlic toast.

Cornbread & Leek Stuffed Pork Chops

INGREDIENTS:

1 teaspoon olive oil

4 (1-inch-thick) boneless top loin pork chops

Kosher salt and freshly ground black pepper

1 tablespoon unsalted butter

1 leek, sliced, rinsed, and patted dry

3 cups cubed Cornbread (page 67)

1 teaspoon chopped fresh thyme leaves

½ cup Homemade Broth (chicken or vegetable, pages 45 and 46)

⅓ cup Sweet Barbecue Sauce (page 31), plus more for serving

MAKE IT A MEAL

Oven-Roasted Butternut Squash with Brown Butter & Crispy Fried Sage (page 159) or Twice-Baked Sweet Potatoes (page 175)

I'm starting to feel like a broken record when it comes to using the words, "this is so easy!" but, alas, it's true. In this recipe, leftover cornbread is mixed with leeks (sautéed in BUTTER!), fresh thyme, and homemade broth before it gets stuffed into thick-cut pork chops. Then they are slathered in homemade barbecue sauce before going into the oven to bake. I mean . . . c'mon.

SERVES 4 • TOTAL TIME: 45 MINUTES

DIRECTIONS:

- Preheat the oven to 350ºF. Lightly grease a 9 by 13-inch baking pan with the olive oil.

- On the fat side of the pork chop, use a sharp paring knife to make a pocket 2 to 2¹/2 inches wide and 1¹/2 to 1³/4 inches deep. Season the pork chops with a pinch of salt and pepper.

- Meanwhile, in a 10-inch skillet, melt the butter over medium heat. Add the leek and ¹/4 teaspoon of salt and sauté until soft, about 10 minutes.

- In a large bowl, combine the sautéed leek, cornbread, thyme, and broth. Season with ¹/4 teaspoon of salt and pepper. Use a wooden spoon to combine until the mixture resembles wet coarse crumbles.

- Fill each of the pork chops with the stuffing.

- Place the stuffed pork chops into the prepared pan and brush with half the barbecue sauce. Bake for 15 minutes. Remove the pan, increase the oven temperature to 400ºF, and brush the pork chops with the remaining barbecue sauce. Bake for 15 minutes more.

- Serve immediately with extra warmed barbecue sauce on the side.

Beer-Braised Lamb Shanks

Once in a while, I stumble upon lamb shanks in the meat case at my grocery store. It's not often, but when I do, I like to braise them in dark beer with lots of vegetables.

Lamb was one of those things I remember having as a kid on special occasions. I also remember the horrific mint jelly my parents would eat with it. Ugh. As a picky child, I could not deal with that. As a thirty-something-year-old . . . I prefer a gremolata. Which really is only a fancy-pants name for herbs with garlic and lemon zest. Although it sounds gourmet and looks pretty, it's rustic and tastes fantastic with the earthy lamb.

SERVES 6 TO 8 • TOTAL TIME: 3½ TO 4 HOURS

DIRECTIONS:

- To make the lamb: Preheat the oven to 325°F.

- In a large Dutch oven, heat the olive oil over medium-high heat.

- Season all sides of the lamb shanks generously with salt and pepper. Brown the lamb shanks in the Dutch oven for 3 to 4 minutes per side before transferring them to a clean plate.

- Drain off all but 1 tablespoon of the rendered fat from the pot. Add the butter, carrots, celery, onion, and garlic. Cook for 8 to 10 minutes, or until the vegetables have browned.

- Meanwhile, bundle the thyme, parsley, and rosemary tightly with kitchen string.

- Add the flour and tomato paste, stir to combine, and cook for 3 minutes. Add the beer, broth, herb bundle, and bay leaf. Place the lamb shanks on top of the vegetables—they should not be submerged. You want to leave about ½ inch of the meat exposed. If needed, add more broth or water to the pot.

- Cover the pot and braise in the oven for 2½ to 3 hours.

INGREDIENTS:

FOR THE LAMB:

2 tablespoons olive oil

6 to 8 lamb shanks (depending on size)

2 tablespoons unsalted butter

2 medium carrots, chopped

2 celery stalks, chopped

1 large yellow onion, chopped

4 cloves garlic, smashed

3 sprigs fresh thyme

3 sprigs fresh flat-leaf parsley

2 sprigs fresh rosemary

2 tablespoons unbleached all-purpose flour

2 rounded tablespoons tomato paste

12 ounces dark beer

1½ cups beef broth

1 bay leaf

FOR THE GREMOLATA:

½ cup chopped flat-leaf parsley

¼ cup chopped mint leaves

1 teaspoon minced rosemary leaves

½ teaspoon minced thyme leaves

2 cloves garlic, minced

1 tablespoon lemon zest

- Use tongs to remove the lamb shanks, place them on a clean plate, and tent with aluminum foil. Remove the herb bundle and bay leaf before emulsifying the sauce. This can be done in a blender or directly in the pot using an immersion blender.

- Return the lamb shanks to the pot and cover with a lid. Keep warm over low heat.

- To make the gremolata: In a small bowl, combine the parsley, mint, rosemary, thyme, garlic, and zest.

- Serve the lamb shanks with a spoonful of the gremolata on top of the lamb.

MAKE IT A MEAL

Curried Cauliflower with Golden Raisins & Pistachios (page 203), Roasted Beets with Parsley Pesto Vinaigrette (page 169), Roasted Garlic Whipped Cauliflower (page 166), or Dijon Roasted Brussels Sprouts (page 191)

Skirt Steak Fajitas

One of the first meals I recall making for my husband in our early years of marriage was fajitas. It was our go-to meal at the time, and when I say we made it *all* the time, I really do mean all the time. We thought we were so gourmet with our box of store-bought, frozen, precooked, preseasoned, presliced, even, and pregrilled fajita chicken strips, served with a bag of frozen fajita vegetables. ***cringe*** For real! How could I? I shake my head, even all these years later.

Now when I make fajitas, I like to pull out all the stops. (I'm still making up for my fajita-related crimes.) It takes five minutes to whip up this super-flavorful thirty-minute marinade, and while the steak is marinating, I quickly cook up onions and peppers, Skillet Refried Black Beans, and my kids' favorite, 5-Minute Avocado Spread.

It all comes together in a harmonious union of flavors, flavors that you can't find in any premade package or box at the store. We all love this recipe so much that I make it at least three times a month (it's more like four or five, if I'm being honest), and it never, *ever* gets old.

Bonus: This recipe can also be made with boneless, skinless chicken breasts. Cooking the chicken just takes a little longer than the steak, but it's equally as delicious.

MAKES 14 TO 16 FAJITAS • TOTAL TIME: ABOUT 1 HOUR 10 MINUTES

DIRECTIONS:

- In a shallow bowl, combine the garlic, fajita seasoning, grape-seed oil, and cilantro. Toss the steak to coat in the marinade. Cover and marinate for 30 minutes.

- Meanwhile, heat a 12-inch cast-iron skillet over medium-high heat. Place the butter, olive oil, and onion in the skillet. Season with the salt, stir, and cook until the edges of the onion

INGREDIENTS:

1 clove garlic, minced

1 recipe Fajita (or Taco) Seasoning (page 39 or 40; see Simply Scratch Tip)

¼ cup grape-seed or olive oil

¼ cup fresh cilantro leaves, chopped, plus more for serving

1 ½ pounds skirt steak, halved crosswise

2 tablespoons unsalted butter

1 tablespoon olive oil

1 sweet onion, halved and sliced vertically

½ teaspoon kosher salt

½ red bell pepper, sliced into strips

½ orange bell pepper, sliced into strips

2 wedges of lime

TO SERVE:

Skillet Refried Black Beans (page 195)

Pico de Gallo (page 81)

5-Minute Avocado Spread (page 80)

1 cup Cotija cheese

16 warm tortillas

My kids find it hard to bite into the steak strips, so for the second round in the pan I sometimes chop it up into even smaller pieces. Also, if you are using the taco seasoning, add 1 tablespoon cornstarch to the marinade. It will help make a delicious crust on the outside of the steak (or chicken).

are deeply golden yet still a bit firm, about 10 minutes. Add the peppers and cook for 5 to 8 minutes more, depending on how done you want them. Transfer the onion and peppers to a small dish.

- Working in two batches, sear the steak on both sides for 3 to 4 minutes on each side. Transfer to a cutting board and let rest for 5 to 8 minutes before slicing into thin strips. Return the strips and any juices from the cutting board to the skillet, squeeze in the juice from the lime wedges, and cook for 3 to 4 minutes more. Remove from the heat and tent with aluminum foil to keep warm.

- On a warm tortilla, spread a spoonful of refried beans and top with steak, onions and peppers, avocado spread, Cotija cheese, and more cilantro, if desired.

MAKE IT A MEAL

Again, these are terrific served with Skillet Refried Black Beans (page 195), Pico de Gallo (page 81), and 5-Minute Avocado Spread (page 80).

Spaghetti & Meatballs

My favorite part of making spaghetti and meatballs is the moment I need to "test" a meatball, you know, to "make sure" they're completely cooked through (wink!). Every time I test them, I work to convince myself that I don't even need the spaghetti; I could just eat a bowlful of meatballs covered in the sauce. But being a glutton for all things carbs, I go for the spaghetti every time. It's okay, though, because I can always make up for it next time.

These meatballs are flavorful, moist, and a little healthier, thanks to the addition of ground turkey. Homemade marinara: check. Homemade meatballs: check. One comforting, delicious, family-style dinner: check, check.

SERVES 4 TO 6 • TOTAL TIME: 1 HOUR 20 MINUTES

DIRECTIONS:

- In a large bowl, combine the beef, turkey, egg, shallot, garlic, parsley, bread crumbs, and Parmesan. Use a fork to mix until all the ingredients are incorporated; do not overmix.

- Measure out rounded tablespoons of the mixture and roll them into roughly 38 meatballs.

- Heat a 12-inch skillet over medium heat. Add the olive oil. Working in batches, brown the meatballs for 3 to 4 minutes on all sides. Remove them and place them on a clean platter. Repeat with the remaining meatballs.

- Pour in the marinara and bring to a simmer. Reduce the heat to low and simmer for 20 to 25 minutes. Return the meatballs to the sauce, stir to coat, and heat them for 5 to 10 minutes, or until fully cooked. This is where I scoop out a meatball to "test," like I mentioned earlier.

- Meanwhile, bring a large pot of water to a boil and cook the spaghetti according to the package directions.

INGREDIENTS:

FOR THE MEATBALLS:

¾ pound ground beef chuck

¾ pound ground turkey

1 large egg, lightly beaten

⅓ cup minced shallot

2 cloves garlic, minced

2 tablespoons minced fresh flat-leaf parsley

¾ cup Italian-Seasoned Bread Crumbs (page 58)

¼ cup freshly grated Parmesan cheese, plus more for serving

1 teaspoon olive oil

1 recipe Classic Marinara (page 78)

¾ pound dried spaghetti

- Serve the spaghetti in bowls topped with the meatballs, sauce, and lots of grated Parmesan!

SIMPLY SCRATCH TIP

When I make the marinara fresh for this recipe, I omit the tablespoon of oil in the marinara recipe and sauté the shallot and garlic in the fat left over from the meatballs.

MAKE IT A MEAL

Try it with Roasted Eggplant & Tomato Panzanella (page 139).

Grilled Rib-Eye Steaks with Mushroom-Shallot Butter

I'm a firm believer that a great steak only needs salt and pepper . . . annnnnd a heavenly compound butter. Enough said. This one's as amazing as it sounds.

SERVES 4 TO 6 • TOTAL TIME: 35 MINUTES TO 1 HOUR

INGREDIENTS:

8 tablespoons (1 stick) plus 3 tablespoons unsalted butter, at room temperature

½ cup sliced shallot

Heaping 1 cup sliced cremini mushrooms

2 large cloves garlic, minced

1 teaspoon coarsely chopped fresh thyme leaves

¼ teaspoon kosher salt, plus more as needed

¼ teaspoon coarsely ground black pepper, plus more as needed

4 to 6 steaks (such as rib-eye, New York strip, or porterhouse)

MAKE IT A MEAL

Serve with Parsnip Fries (page 163) or Baked Beans (page 183).

DIRECTIONS:

- Melt 1 tablespoon of the butter in a medium skillet over medium-low heat. Add the shallot and cook until golden and slightly crispy, 7 to 8 minutes. Use a slotted spoon to transfer the shallot to a clean plate. In the same skillet, melt 2 tablespoons of butter, then add the mushrooms, garlic, thyme, salt, and pepper. Stir and cook until the mushrooms are softened, about 5 minutes. Transfer to the plate with the shallot and let cool.

- In a small bowl, use a rubber spatula to blend the remaining 8 tablespoons of butter with the cooled mushroom mixture until combined.

- Place the butter in the center of a piece of parchment paper. Bring the edges together and press with your fingers to form the butter into a log. Roll and twist the ends before popping the butter into the fridge for at least 20 to 30 minutes. (When I'm in a pinch, I stick it in the freezer.)

- Set the steaks on the counter for 30 minutes to bring them up to room temperature. Meanwhile, preheat a grill or grill pan to medium-high or about 400°F. Season both sides of the steaks with 2 pinches of salt and a pinch of pepper.

- Grill each steak for 6 to 8 minutes per side, depending on the thickness and desired doneness. Tent with aluminum foil and let rest for 5 minutes.

- Slice the mushroom butter into coins and top each of the steaks with two coins before serving.

One-Pot Autumnal Beef Stew

As the weather cools and the leaves start to turn, it's as if a switch flicks and I'm instantly craving comfort food. Fall is my favorite season of all, and if I'm not braising big hunks of meat, then I'm enjoying bowls of chili or a warm stew loaded with tender pieces of beef and root vegetables swimming in a rich brown sauce.

This is a stew that has all my favorite fall vegetables like parsnips, butternut squash, and turnips. It fills my home with a truly amazing aroma. Sometimes I purposely leave the house just so I can walk back in and get smacked in the face with it. True story.

This perfect one-pot meal goes perfectly with a thick slice of homemade bread. So naturally, I dig it.

SERVES 6 • TOTAL TIME: 3 HOURS 25 MINUTES

DIRECTIONS:

- Toss the cubed beef with ¾ teaspoon of both the salt and pepper. Add the flour and toss until the beef is lightly coated.

- Heat a large Dutch oven over medium-high heat. Once it's hot, heat 1 tablespoon of the olive oil. Working in batches, sear one-third of the beef on all sides until a deep golden crust forms, 3 to 4 minutes per side. Remove and repeat with the remaining beef and oil in two more batches. Transfer all the beef to a clean platter and set aside.

- Add the diced onion to the Dutch oven and cook for 5 minutes, or until just soft. Add the garlic and tomato paste and cook for 1 minute.

- Pour in the wine, scraping up the browned bits on the bottom of the pot. Add the currants and browned beef and pour in the broth. Season with the remaining ½ teaspoon salt and pepper. Stir and bring to a boil, reduce the heat to maintain a simmer, cover, and cook for 50 minutes.

INGREDIENTS:

2½ pounds bottom round roast, cut into 1-inch cubes

1¼ teaspoons kosher salt

1¼ teaspoons coarsely ground black pepper

¼ cup unbleached all-purpose flour or cornstarch

3 tablespoons olive oil

1 large yellow onion, chopped

2 cloves garlic, smashed

2 tablespoons tomato paste

1 cup dry red wine (like merlot, or substitute with additional broth)

¼ cup dried currants

4 cups beef broth

3 carrots, cut on an angle into ½-inch-thick slices

2 cups butternut squash, peeled and cut into ½-inch pieces

1 medium turnip, peeled and cut into ½-inch pieces

1½ cups quartered cremini mushrooms

2 tablespoons minced fresh flat-leaf parsley, for garnish

- Remove the lid, stir, and bring back to a boil for 30 minutes. Add the carrots, squash, turnip, and mushrooms. Add water or more broth if the vegetables are not completely submerged. Cover and cook for 25 minutes, or until the vegetables are fork-tender. Serve in a big bowl with minced parsley sprinkled over the top.

MAKE IT A MEAL

Enjoy this with Easy French Bread (page 54) or Cornbread (page 67), or try it spooned over Roasted Garlic Whipped Cauliflower (page 166).

Cottage Pie

Whether you call it cottage pie or shepherd's pie, I firmly believe this is a universally loved dish. Meat, tender vegetables, and potatoes—you really can't go wrong.

While you could most definitely use ground lamb in this recipe, I prefer ground round. I also love adding lots of veggies and making a thick, dark, "gravy"-like sauce. Once you've made the filling, it goes into a baking dish and you spoon creamy cheddar mashed potatoes over the top before sliding it into a hot oven. As it bakes, the exposed top and edges of the potato get crispy. I am *all* about those crispy edges.

The smell alone as it cooks is like a hug that you don't want to break away from. Eating it is soul warming, comforting, and oh-so-very filling.

SERVES 6 • TOTAL TIME: 1 HOUR 35 MINUTES

DIRECTIONS:

- To make the filling: In a Dutch oven, melt the butter over medium-low heat. Add the onion, carrot, and celery. Stir to coat the vegetables in the butter, cover, and cook, stirring occasionally, for 15 minutes, until soft. Add the garlic and cook for 1 to 2 minutes more. Use a spoon to transfer the cooked vegetables to a bowl.

- In the Dutch oven, cook the ground beef over medium heat, breaking it into small crumbles as it cooks, until cooked through. Return the vegetables to the pot and stir in the tomato paste and flour. Pour in the wine and cook for 2 to 3 minutes. Pour in the broth and Worcestershire and add the thyme sprigs and bay leaf. Season with salt and pepper and cook, stirring occasionally, for 30 minutes. Stir in the peas and pour the filling into a 3- to 4-quart baking dish.

- While the filling is cooking, make the mashed potatoes: Preheat the oven to 400°F.

INGREDIENTS:

FOR THE FILLING:

3 tablespoons unsalted butter

2 cups diced yellow onion

1 cup diced carrot

1 cup diced celery

3 cloves garlic, minced

2½ pounds ground round

2 tablespoons tomato paste

2 tablespoons unbleached all-purpose flour

¼ cup pinot noir (or any good dry red wine)

2 cups beef broth

¼ cup Worcestershire sauce

4 sprigs fresh thyme

1 bay leaf

1½ teaspoons kosher salt

½ teaspoon freshly ground black pepper

½ cup frozen peas

FOR THE MASHED POTATOES:

3½ pounds russet potatoes, peeled and cut into large pieces

Kosher salt

1¼ cups whole milk

4 tablespoons unsalted butter

¾ cup grated sharp white cheddar cheese

1 tablespoon minced fresh flat-leaf parsley

1 teaspoon chopped fresh thyme leaves

Try using sweet potatoes instead of russets, for a healthier option and a pop of color.

- Place the peeled potatoes in a pot and add cold water to cover by about 2 inches. Add a generous pinch of salt, cover, and bring to a boil. Crack the lid and cook the potatoes for 15 to 20 minutes, or until fork-tender.

- With the lid askew, carefully drain the water from the pot with the potatoes. Return the pot to the stove over low heat. Add the milk and butter to the potatoes, cover, and simmer the potatoes in the milk and butter for 10 to 12 minutes. Season the potatoes with ¾ teaspoon of salt and mash with a potato masher or mix with a hand mixer. Add the cheddar and stir to combine. Taste and season with more salt if needed.

- Use a spatula to spoon the mashed potatoes over the filling in the baking dish and spread them out evenly. Use a fork and drag it along the top of the mashed potatoes to make ridges. These will crisp up and brown in the oven.

- Place the cottage pie on a rimmed baking sheet and slide it into the oven. Bake for 20 minutes, or until the top of the potatoes is golden and crispy and the filling is bubbling.

- Combine the minced parsley and thyme.

- Serve large spoonfuls of the cottage pie in bowls with a sprinkle of the parsley and thyme.

MAKE IT A MEAL

This main dish is an all-in-one, so I typically serve it with a crisp garden salad and warm rolls or Buttermilk Biscuits (page 62).

Blackberry-Glazed Salmon

Patience has never been my strong suit. I can admit it. And boy, was my patience thinning big time when I was creating this recipe. After many trials and many errors, I was determined to survive and give you the blackberry-lacquered salmon I had originally envisioned—and I've delivered.

The key to making this lustrous blackberry, ginger, and lime glaze is to reduce, reduce, and reduce! Don't add a cornstarch slurry . . . do not think, hope, and wish it will thicken up under the broiler. Nope and nope. It took me several attempts to realize I just needed a little more patience for the glaze to thicken on the stove, and now I'm pretty darn positive that this may be my favorite salmon recipe to date.

The sweetness of the glaze shellacs itself to the salmon and complements the fish and its rich texture beautifully. It's just SO good! And the sky is the limit in the many ways you can serve this: put it on a salad, alongside rice or quinoa, or with your favorite vegetables. It's healthy, light, and so darn pretty.

SERVES 4 • TOTAL TIME: 45 MINUTES

DIRECTIONS:

- Peel the ginger with a knife, slice it into 4 coins, and smash each with the knife's blunt end. Place the ginger, berries, lime juice, and ¼ cup water in a small saucepan. Bring to a boil, reduce the heat to medium-low, and simmer for 10 to 12 minutes, or until the blackberries are soft and start to fall apart easily. Pour the blackberries and liquids through a mesh strainer set over a bowl and use a spoon to press the mixture through. Discard the berry solids.

- Return the blackberry liquid to the saucepan, stir in the sugar and lime zest, and bring back to a boil. Reduce the heat to medium-low and simmer until the liquid has reduced to about ¼ cup, 20 to 25 minutes.

INGREDIENTS:

1 (1½-inch) piece fresh ginger

6 ounces fresh blackberries

Zest and juice of 1 lime

2 tablespoons dark brown sugar

Olive oil

4 (6-ounce) fresh Atlantic salmon fillets

½ teaspoon kosher salt

¼ teaspoon cracked black pepper

Sliced scallions, for serving

Torn fresh cilantro leaves, for serving

- Meanwhile, preheat the oven to 400ºF. Line a baking sheet with aluminum foil and lightly oil the foil. Arrange the salmon skin-side down on the baking sheet and season with salt and pepper. Bake for 5 minutes. Remove, raise the oven rack to the highest position, and turn the oven to broil. Brush the salmon with the blackberry glaze and broil for 6 minutes, or until the fish is opaque and flakes easily, rotating the pan halfway through to ensure even cooking.

- Top with sliced scallions and torn cilantro and serve immediately.

MAKE IT A MEAL

This salmon is excellent served with Wild Rice & Orzo Pilaf with Dried Cherries & Almonds (page 187).

Broiled Chili-Lime-Crusted Tilapia

I'm completely smitten with this recipe because of its simplicity and incredible flavor. The combination of six pantry spices and lime juice gives the tilapia a crispy crust as it cooks under the broiler. With one final squeeze of lime and torn fresh cilantro, the majority of dinner is cooked in 20 minutes or less. Talk about quick.

I have to confess, over the years I've become somewhat of a fish snob. I don't mind buying frozen shrimp and maybe a few types of frozen fish, but buying fresh tilapia is a total must for me. In my opinion, the texture is completely different and the fish tastes infinitely better. If you can't get your hands on fresh tilapia, frozen will do, of course, or you could try this chili-lime concoction on other seafood like barramundi, cod, or shrimp. It's all good.

Yum.

SERVES 4 • TOTAL TIME: 20 MINUTES

DIRECTIONS:

- Place the oven rack in the top portion of the oven. Crack the oven door and preheat the broiler to high. Line a rimmed baking sheet with aluminum foil and lightly brush the foil with olive oil.

- In a shallow dish, combine the olive oil, lime juice, cornstarch, chili powder, coriander, cumin, oregano, garlic powder, onion powder, salt, and pepper. Whisk to blend.

- Dip both sides of each tilapia fillet into the spice mixture and use your fingers to coat evenly. Place the tilapia on the prepared baking sheet with the bottom facing up. Broil for 4 minutes, then carefully flip and cook for 4 to 5 minutes more, or until the fish flakes easily.

- Serve with lime wedges and torn cilantro or top with a few spoonfuls of Pico de Gallo (page 81).

INGREDIENTS:

2 tablespoons olive oil, plus more for the pan

Juice of 1 lime (about 2 tablespoons)

1 tablespoon cornstarch

1 tablespoon chili powder

1 teaspoon ground coriander

1 teaspoon ground cumin

1 teaspoon dried oregano, rubbed in your palm

½ teaspoon garlic powder

½ teaspoon onion powder

¾ teaspoon kosher salt

¼ teaspoon freshly ground black pepper

4 fresh tilapia fillets

GARNISH:

Lime wedges

Torn fresh cilantro leaves

Pico de Gallo (page 81)

MAKE IT A MEAL

This fish is great with Corn & Jalapeño Sauté (page 179), Skillet Refried Black Beans (page 195), or Fajita Vegetable Stir-Fry (page 197).

Pepita-Crusted Halibut
with Fresh Grape Salsa

This colorful recipe is light, fresh, and flavorful and can be prepared in very few minutes. Both seeds and nuts are terrific chopped or ground into a fine crumb crust for seafood or poultry. It's a healthy way to add texture and crunch, and a nice break from the typical bread crumb routine.

You can find find lightly salted, roasted pepitas in bulk at most grocery stores. I always keep them on hand.

P.S. Grape salsa is totally a thing. I may not eat it with tortilla chips, but this fresh salsa is amazing over this fish. Give it a try!

SERVES 4 • TOTAL TIME: 35 MINUTES

DIRECTIONS:

- To make the fresh grape salsa: In a medium bowl, combine all the ingredients. Toss, cover, and refrigerate until ready to serve.

- To make the pepita-crusted halibut: In a shallow bowl, whisk the egg white until frothy. In a separate shallow dish, spread the pepitas. Season both sides of the halibut with salt and pepper.

- Dip each fillet in the egg white, letting any excess drip back into the bowl. Place the fish in the dish with the pepitas and press the fish so they stick on all sides. Repeat with the remaining fillets.

- In a 12-inch nonstick skillet, heat the oil over medium to medium-high heat. Once hot, place the fillets in the pan and

INGREDIENTS:

FOR THE FRESH GRAPE SALSA:

2 cups quartered red seedless grapes

1 small plum (Roma) tomato, seeded and diced

2 scallions, dark and light green parts only, sliced

2 tablespoons finely diced red onion

1 tablespoon minced fresh cilantro

Juice of ½ lime

¼ teaspoon kosher salt

FOR THE PEPITA-CRUSTED HALIBUT:

1 egg white, beaten

1½ cups coarsely chopped raw pepitas

4 (6-ounce) halibut fillets

Kosher salt and freshly ground black pepper

2 tablespoons grape-seed oil

cook for 3 to 4 minutes per side, or until the fish is opaque and flakes easily. Adjust the heat so you don't burn the pepitas.

· Top with chilled grape salsa and serve with a glass of wine!

MAKE IT A MEAL

Corn & Jalapeño Sauté (page 179), Curried Cauliflower with Golden Raisins & Pistachios (page 203), or Farro Fried "Rice" (page 176)

Vegetarian Potpie

I wish I could take total credit for this recipe concept, but alas, I got my inspiration from yet another restaurant I frequently go to. However, it's not like they hand over their recipe to me and say, "Go for it, Laurie!" I've ordered their vegetarian potpie for years, and each time I try to pick out and guess the flavors. Eventually, I cracked their secret potpie code!

This dish is *filled* with vegetables like parsnips, turnips, and kale, and even the "gravy" is made from pureed sweet potatoes thinned out with homemade vegetable broth. The base is a homemade Vegetable Broth (page 46). This potpie tastes exactly like my beloved dish except I added a delicious twist: an herbed pie crust. Take that.

SERVES 4 TO 6 • TOTAL TIME: 1 HOUR 40 MINUTES

DIRECTIONS:

- Preheat the oven to 400°F.

- Place the sweet potatoes on a small rimmed baking sheet and bake for 45 minutes to 1 hour, or until a fork pierces them without resistance. Remove and let cool. Combine the parsnips, turnips, and 1 tablespoon of the olive oil on a large baking sheet and roast for 25 minutes or until tender. Keep the oven on.

- In a deep 12-inch skillet, sauté the shallot and garlic in 1 teaspoon of the olive oil over medium heat until tender, 5 to 6 minutes.

- Spoon the flesh out of the sweet potatoes and place it in a blender or the bowl of a food processor. Add the shallots, garlic, paprika, salt, and pepper. Add the broth and puree until ultra-smooth. Pour the sweet potato puree into the skillet and add the roasted parsnips and turnips and the kale. Stir to combine and let cool.

- Grease a 2-quart oval or round baking dish with the remaining ½ teaspoon olive oil.

INGREDIENTS:

2 to 2½ pounds sweet potatoes or yams, scrubbed clean

2 medium parsnips, peeled and cut into 1-inch dice

2 medium turnips, peeled and cut into 1-inch dice

1 tablespoon plus 1½ teaspoons olive oil

1 cup diced shallots

2 cloves garlic, minced

1¼ teaspoons smoked paprika

1½ teaspoons kosher salt

½ teaspoon coarsely ground black pepper

2½ cups Vegetable Broth (page 46)

2 cups chopped kale leaves

1 large egg

2 tablespoons whole milk or water

1 recipe Herbed Pie Crust (1 disc; page 50)

- In a small bowl, use a fork to beat the egg and milk. Using a pastry brush, brush the egg mixture on the outside top edge of the baking dish. Then add the cooled vegetable filling.

- Roll out the herbed pie crust and carefully drape it over the filling, pressing the edges so they stick to the egg-washed edge. Brush the egg wash over the entire pie crust before making a few slits for steam to vent.

- Bake for 18 to 22 minutes, or until the filling is bubbling and the crust is a deep golden brown.

- Let the potpie cool slightly before serving.

MAKE IT A MEAL

This potpie is loaded with so much healthful goodness that you may not need a side dish. I usually serve it with a light salad or Adobo Green Beans with Toasted Garlicky Almonds (page 171).

Vegetable Pesto Pizza

If you were to tell my ten-year-old self that my future thirty-something self would fall madly in love with a veggie pizza, I probably would've laughed in your face. From the age of five to eighteen, there was no way I would have put a piece of pizza like this in my mouth, ever. It kind of makes me want to shake that little girl and yell at her to wake up and smell the veggie pesto pizza!

This pizza, with its whole wheat crust, homemade basil pesto, and lots of vegetables and cheese, is delicious pizza perfection, and you definitely won't miss the pepperoni. At all.

Don't believe me? I wouldn't have either, at least not until I tried *this* pizza.

SERVES 4 TO 6 • TOTAL TIME: 30 MINUTES

DIRECTIONS:

- Preheat the oven to 450ºF. Position the rack in the bottom third. Lightly oil a standard round pizza pan.

- On a lightly floured work surface, roll or stretch the dough to fit the pan.

- Spread ½ cup of pesto onto the dough, leaving a ½-inch border around the edge. Top the pesto with zucchini, yellow squash, broccoli, tomatoes, bell pepper, and onion before sprinkling evenly with the mozzarella and Fontina. Lightly brush the crust with olive oil before sliding the pizza into the oven.

- Bake for 15 to 18 minutes, or until the cheeses are melted and the crust is golden brown.

- Sprinkle with red pepper flakes and grated Parmesan.

INGREDIENTS:

Olive oil

Unbleached all-purpose flour, for dusting

1 recipe Whole Wheat Pizza Dough (page 53)

½ cup Basil Pesto (page 33)

½ small zucchini, cut into ¼-inch-thick slices (or ½ cup)

½ small yellow squash, cut into ¼-inch-thick slices (or ½ cup)

1 cup small broccoli florets

1 cup halved cherry tomatoes

1 orange bell pepper, seeded and sliced into rings

1 small red onion, cut into ⅛-inch-thick rounds

2 cups freshly grated mozzarella cheese

1 cup freshly grated Fontina

Red pepper flakes (optional)

Grated Parmesan (optional)

Making the dough and prepping the veggies the night before will save you so much time. All you'll have to do is roll out the dough (and be sure to pull the dough out a little in advance so it can warm to room temperature), assemble the toppings, and you'll be in pizza heaven in less than 30 minutes.

MAKE IT A MEAL

Try it with a Classic Greek Salad (page 142).

CHAPTER SEVEN

Desserts

Saving room for dessert has never been an issue for me. I was the kid stealing all of the Hershey's Kisses off the peanut butter blossom cookies from my grandma's Christmas dessert table (sorry, Grandma, that was me!). When we visited my dad for the weekend, my sister Julie and I would return his pop cans at the corner store to collect the 10 cents per can refund and then blow it on sugar: Bazooka gum, 5-cent candies, candy bars, and pop. I basically OD'd on sugar every other weekend. Yet I would scrape the frosting off a slice of birthday cake before eating it. Riddle me that.

Now I'm the adult who orders tiramisu with her after-dinner cup of coffee. Though it pains me, I'll even split a slice of raspberry cheesecake with my husband. Dessert is a well-loved fourth meal in our house.

This dessert chapter is filled with all my favorite desserts to make *and*, of course, eat. They are simple and will satisfy any sweet tooth. If you're in the mood for a chewy, chocolaty, nutty, and a smidge salty cookie, then try the Salted Pistachio Dark Chocolate Chunk Cookies (page 271). Or maybe you want something light, creamy, and lemony (because who wouldn't?). Turn to my Lemon Lavender Crème Brûlée (page 273). It's hard to resist breaking the sugar crust with your spoon and diving in, trust me. Whether it's a classic like a freshly baked pie or a spin on a beloved summer treat, this chapter won't let you down.

Desserts

Fudgy Chocolate Toffee-Topped Brownies

Once, at my good friend Heidi's house, I sampled brownies that would change my life. Forever.

They were super-fudgy, not-overly-rich brownies topped with English toffee. SO simple and something her family has done for years. Now they are something I make *all the time*. Birthday, Christmas . . . Monday, Tuesday . . . you name it. They are a crowd-pleaser.

For this recipe, I took my go-to brownie recipe, added vanilla and cinnamon to the batter, and topped them with English toffee. The brownie becomes one with the toffee in the most amazingly fudgy, crunchy-chocolate-toffee brownie way, leaving you in a state of pure bliss. Oh, and my key to decadent fudgy brownies? I slightly underbake them. I pull the brownies out of the oven when the cake tester comes out with a trace of brownie batter still clinging to it. The brownies continue to bake a bit once they're out of the oven, and the end result is perfection. Even more amazing, these brownies only taste better the next day, as the gooey insides become even more delicious.

MAKES 1 (8 BY 8-INCH) PAN OR ABOUT 9 BROWNIES • TOTAL TIME: 1 HOUR

DIRECTIONS:

- Preheat the oven to 350ºF. Grease an 8 by 8-inch metal baking pan with 1 tablespoon of the butter and line it with parchment paper, leaving an inch of the parchment paper hanging over on two sides.

- In a medium saucepan, melt the chocolate and remaining 8 tablespoons butter over low heat, stirring often. Once melted, remove from the heat and add the sugars and vanilla. Stir and set aside to cool slightly.

INGREDIENTS:

8 tablespoons (1 stick) plus 1 tablespoon unsalted butter, cut into pieces

8 ounces bittersweet chocolate, chopped into pieces

1 cup granulated sugar

¾ cup packed dark brown sugar

½ teaspoon pure vanilla extract

1¼ cups unbleached all-purpose flour

⅓ cup unsweetened cocoa powder

½ teaspoon baking powder

½ teaspoon ground cinnamon

½ teaspoon kosher salt

4 large eggs, at room temperature

2 cups toffee bits

Vanilla Bean Ice Cream (page 269), for serving

- In a large bowl, sift the flour, cocoa powder, baking powder, cinnamon, and salt and set aside.

- To the slightly warm chocolate, add the eggs one at a time, whisking after each addition. Pour the chocolate mixture into the flour mixture, using a spatula or wooden spoon to stir until combined.

- Pour the batter into the prepared pan and sprinkle evenly with the toffee bits. Bake for 45 to 50 minutes, or until a tester comes out slightly coated with a thicker coat of chocolate batter after it's inserted into the center (it shouldn't be runny).

- Let the brownies cool in the pan for 1 hour before running a knife along the edges. Then use the parchment paper as handles to remove. Cut into squares and serve with Vanilla Bean Ice Cream.

Rustic Blueberry Peach Crisp

This crisp blows my mind. Not only is blueberry and peach one of my favorite fruit combinations in the whole wide world, but the oatmeal pecan topping in this recipe is amazingly versatile, too. (Translation: Sprinkle it on your ice cream, in puddings—anything that's soft and you want to give a little texture to.) It's seriously *that* good.

SERVES 6 TO 8 • TOTAL TIME: 50 MINUTES

DIRECTIONS:

• Preheat the oven to 350°F. Grease an 8 by 8-inch or 2-quart glass baking dish with the butter.

• To make the topping: In a medium bowl, use a wooden spoon to combine all the ingredients. Set aside.

• To make the filling: In a large bowl, combine the flour, brown sugar, cinnamon, cardamom, ginger, lemon juice, and vanilla. Add the peaches and blueberries and gently toss to combine.

• Pour the fruit into the prepared pan. Pinch small amounts of the oat topping into clumps and scatter over the filling. Bake for 30 to 40 minutes, until the fruit is tender and the liquids are bubbling.

• Let cool slightly before serving. Use a slotted spoon to serve the crisp into small bowls and top with a scoop of Vanilla Bean Ice Cream.

SIMPLY SCRATCH TIP

When using frozen peaches, do NOT thaw them. Thawing will unleash a flood of juices in the pan when the crisp is baking.

INGREDIENTS:

1 tablespoon unsalted butter, at room temperature

FOR THE TOPPING:

½ cup chopped pecans

½ cup quick-cooking oats

½ cup packed dark brown sugar

½ teaspoon ground cinnamon

⅛ teaspoon kosher salt

3 tablespoons unsalted butter, at room temperature

FOR THE FILLING:

¼ cup unbleached all-purpose flour

¼ cup packed light brown sugar

1 teaspoon ground cinnamon

¼ teaspoon ground cardamom

⅛ teaspoon ground ginger

1 teaspoon fresh lemon juice

1 teaspoon pure vanilla extract

4 cups frozen sliced peaches (peeled or unpeeled)

1 pint (or 2 cups) fresh blueberries

Vanilla Bean Ice Cream (page 269), for serving

Vanilla Bean Ice Cream

Double the vanilla. Doubly delicious. One extremely easy vanilla bean ice cream. This recipe requires an ice cream maker. If you don't have one, I'd seriously recommend buying one right away—besides using it for this recipe, making ice cream is loads of fun and a great family activity. My girls and I always love hanging out and making ice cream together.

MAKES 1 QUART • TOTAL TIME: 1 HOUR 5 MINUTES PLUS 4 HOURS TO OVERNIGHT COOLING TIME

DIRECTIONS:

- In a large bowl with a pour spout, whisk together the cream, half-and-half, sugar, vanilla, and sea salt until the sugar has dissolved. Split the vanilla bean in half lengthwise and use the back of your knife to scrape out the seeds. Add the vanilla bean seeds plus the pod to the cream mixture, stir, cover, and chill in the refrigerator for 1 hour.

- Remove and discard the pod before pouring the ice cream base into your ice cream maker and blend until thick according to the manufacturer's instructions. Transfer the ice cream into a freezer-safe container and freeze for 4 hours to overnight.

- Set the ice cream out to soften for 20 minutes prior to scooping and serving.

INGREDIENTS:

2 cups heavy cream

2 cups half-and-half

1 cup sugar

1 tablespoon pure vanilla extract

Pinch of sea salt

1 large vanilla bean

Salted Pistachio
Dark Chocolate Chunk Cookies

I made these cookies the night before my friend Heidi and I went on a mini road trip way across town to go vintage antique shopping. The morning of, I packed a container to take with us, and I'm so glad I did. Not only did these cookies make a great midmorning snack to go with our coffees, but I was eager for her to try them because we both are lovers of all things dark chocolate. Her exact words were, "These are salty-sweet-cookie heaven." I think she's 100 percent correct.

If heaven has a dessert table, I bet these would be on it.

MAKES 3 DOZEN • TOTAL TIME: ABOUT 1 HOUR

DIRECTIONS:

- Preheat the oven to 375ºF. Line two baking sheets with parchment paper or silicone baking mats.

- In a medium bowl, whisk together the flour, baking powder, baking soda, and salt. Set aside.

- In the bowl of a stand mixer fitted with the paddle attachment, cream together the butter and both sugars on medium-low speed for 2 to 3 minutes or until fluffy. Add the eggs one at a time, mixing after each addition. Scrape down the sides and bottom of the bowl after each egg. Add the vanilla and blend until combined.

- With the mixer running on low speed, gradually add the flour mixture and mix until the flour is incorporated. Add the chopped dark chocolate and pistachios to the batter. Mix on low until combined, scraping the sides and bottom of the bowl one last time.

INGREDIENTS:

2¼ cups unbleached all-purpose flour

1 teaspoon baking powder

¾ teaspoon baking soda

¾ teaspoon kosher salt

8 tablespoons (1 stick) unsalted butter

⅔ cup packed dark brown sugar

⅔ cup granulated sugar

2 large eggs

1 teaspoon pure vanilla extract

4 ounces dark chocolate (I use 60% cacao), chopped

¾ cup coarsely chopped pistachios

1 tablespoon flaky sea salt, or more to taste

- Using a 2-tablespoon scoop, scoop out the cookie dough onto the prepared baking sheets, spacing the scoops an inch or so apart. Sprinkle them with a small pinch of sea salt.

- Bake the cookies for 8 to 10 minutes, rotating the baking sheets halfway through. Let the cookies cool slightly, 2 to 3 minutes, before using a spatula to transfer them to a wire rack to finish cooling.

Lemon Lavender Crème Brûlée

The first time I had crème brûlée was a euphoric moment. Breaking through the caramelized sugar layer to get to the cool, creamy custard—bliss. That experience made me wonder just how hard it could be to make it. Turns out, not hard at all. Although my right arm felt as if it would fall off after whisking the six egg yolks for what seemed like forever, the end result is so totally worth it. Plus, the whisking technically counts as exercise (wink wink).

There is this ever-so-faint floral touch from the lavender that works harmoniously with the lemon here. I could eat all six servings in one sitting without batting an eye. And I almost did. There are worse things in life, right?

SERVES 6 • TOTAL TIME: 55 MINUTES PLUS OVERNIGHT

DIRECTIONS:

- Preheat the oven to 325ºF.

- Place the egg yolks and granulated sugar in a large bowl and whisk until thick and light yellow in color. Add the vanilla and stir.

- Pour the cream into a medium saucepan. Add the grated zest, lavender, and salt. Heat over medium-low heat, stirring occasionally, until it is just about to boil. Watch carefully. Immediately remove from the heat and pour through a fine-mesh strainer set over a 4-cup liquid measuring cup.

- While whisking, slowly pour a little of the warm cream into the egg yolk mixture to temper the eggs, then pour in the rest of the cream.

- Ladle the custard base into six 1-cup ramekins and arrange them on a roasting pan, then set the pan on the middle rack that has been slightly pulled out of your oven. Carefully fill the roasting pan with enough warm water that it comes half-way up the sides of the ramekins.

INGREDIENTS:

6 large egg yolks

⅓ cup granulated sugar

½ teaspoon pure vanilla extract

3 cups heavy cream

Zest of 2 large lemons

1 tablespoon culinary lavender

Pinch of sea salt

¼ cup superfine sugar

- Bake for 25 to 30 minutes, or until set. Keep a watchful eye on them, as they should not brown. Remove and let cool in the water bath for 10 minutes. When cool enough to handle, carefully transfer them to a rimmed baking sheet and chill in the refrigerator for 3 to 4 hours, or up to overnight.

- Sprinkle each ramekin with 2 teaspoons of ultrafine sugar. Using a kitchen torch, sweep the flame over the top of the sugar until it's caramelized. Wait for the sugar to cool before serving.

SIMPLY SCRATCH TIP

Finding culinary lavender can be somewhat tricky. I buy mine from Penzeys. You can also order it from other online sources.

Mini French Coconut Tarts

Okay, here's the thing: I know there are coconut haters out there who may be about to flip the page, but I just have to stop you. I mean, I get it. I am no fan of imitation coconut, and that's all that most of us have ever had. Unsweetened flaked coconut has a different flavor. If you have coconut haters in your family, try this and change their minds. My husband thinks he doesn't like coconut, but he loves these mini tarts!

This may be the best flipping dessert ever to be mini-ized (that's totally a word, right?). Here is the story behind these beauties: A few years ago for Christmas, my mother gave my sisters and me a three-ring binder packed with recipes titled "Our Family's Treasury of Favorite Recipes." I took my mom's recipe for French coconut pie and upped the coconut (because I can), and baked them in a mini muffin pan with little rounds of homemade pie crust (page 49). After ten very short minutes in the oven, I hungrily inhaled one of these beauties, burning my taste buds off in the process. Oh, and I may have had a second one on the spot. Did I mention this is a judgment-free cookbook? Well, if I didn't, I do now.

As they bake, the tops get golden and the center remains custardy. Simply put, these tarts are completely unbelievable. And the good news is that if you don't have a mini muffin pan, you can always fill a 9-inch pie crust with this filling. No soul should leave this earth without tasting these. I mean it.

MAKES 34 MINI TARTS • TOTAL TIME: 1 HOUR

INGREDIENTS:

Olive oil mister or nonstick baking spray

1 recipe All-Purpose Crust (2 discs; page 49)

8 tablespoons (1 stick) unsalted butter

3 large eggs

1 cup sugar

1 tablespoon distilled white vinegar

1 teaspoon pure vanilla extract

1¼ cups unsweetened flaked coconut (I like Bob's Red Mill)

⅛ teaspoon kosher salt

DIRECTIONS:

- Preheat the oven to 425ºF. Spray a mini muffin pan with the olive oil mister or baking spray.

- Roll out the pie dough to ⅛ to ¼ inch thick. Use a 2½-inch round biscuit cutter to stamp out 24 rounds. Gently press each circle of dough into each muffin well and refrigerate while making the filling. Wrap the unused dough in plastic wrap and refrigerate that as well.

- Melt the butter in a small saucepan over low heat. Remove and let cool.

- In a medium bowl, whisk together the eggs, sugar, vinegar, vanilla, coconut, and salt. Slowly pour in the cooled melted butter while whisking. Remove the muffin pan from the refrigerator. Use a tablespoon to measure and fill each chilled pie crust with 1 tablespoon of the coconut mixture.

- Bake for 10 minutes. Let the tarts cool in the pan for 10 minutes before transferring them to a wire rack. Repeat with the remaining dough and filling, making 10 more mini tarts.

Homemade New York–Style Cheesecake

I originally found my go-to cheesecake online years before I began blogging. I'd agreed to make a cheesecake at the request of my youngest for her fifth birthday, so I scoured the Internet to find just the right recipe. Back then, I was a little unsure of myself in the kitchen, so I selected one that didn't require a bain-marie (hot water bath), because I knew in my heart of hearts I would screw something up and ruin my daughter's birthday cake.

Over the years, I've made cheesecake a dozen or so times because it's such a hit at get-togethers. I make my own graham crackers for a truly homemade crust, and I've learned a few tricks about the best cheesecake-making technique. The first rule is to make sure all ingredients are at room temperature. They will blend much more easily this way; otherwise, you'll have lumps of cream cheese throughout the mixture. The second rule is to butter that pan like crazy!! Do not be shy, and make sure the bottom and sides are generously covered. It will keep the cheesecake from sticking and decreases the chances of it cracking as it rises in the oven. Butter is your friend. Finally, the third rule, do the dang bain-marie! Your cheesecake will not crack as a result, and it will look gorgeous. (If it cracks, no biggie—obviously, it will still taste amazing!)

There are several factors that may cause a cheesecake to crack: 1) the cheesecake sticks to the pan; 2) it's baking and/or cooling too fast; 3) the oven is dry, i.e., there's no bain-marie. It's easy enough to make a perfect cheesecake just by taking the extra steps I've mentioned. Just keep an eye on it while it's in the oven, and if you notice cracks forming, immediately skip to the cooling step.

If your cheesecake still ends up with surface cracks, cover it with Roasted Maple Strawberry Sauce (page 282), move on, and pretend it never happened. Trust me—when your family and friends try this cheesecake, you won't hear any complaints.

INGREDIENTS:

1 tablespoon unsalted butter

FOR THE CRUST:

10 Honey Graham Crackers (page 60)

4 tablespoons unsalted butter, melted

¼ cup sugar (optional)

FOR THE CHEESECAKE:

4 (8-ounce) packages full-fat cream cheese, at room temperature

1½ cups sugar

¾ cup whole milk, at room temperature

1 cup sour cream, at room temperature

1 tablespoon pure vanilla extract

4 large eggs, at room temperature

¼ cup unbleached all-purpose flour

Roasted Maple Strawberry Sauce (page 282), for serving

Although I think a beautiful crack in the middle gives cheesecake a homemade, rustic look, I understand how some may not share the same sentiment. You'll need to use a bain-marie if you're aiming to have a perfect-looking cheesecake. Here's what to do: Double-wrap the bottom of the springform pan in aluminum foil before making the crust. Once you've pressed the crust in the pan and poured in the cheesecake filling, set the pan in a large roasting pan and fill with 1 inch of hot water before placing it in the oven. The bain-marie will create a saunalike environment in your oven, and fingers crossed, it will also help you make one gorgeous cheesecake.

MAKES ONE 9-INCH CHEESECAKE, TO SERVE 8 TO 10

TOTAL TIME: 5 HOURS TO OVERNIGHT (INCLUDES CHILL TIME)

DIRECTIONS:

- Pull out all the ingredients 20 to 30 minutes prior to making the cheesecake.

- Arrange the oven rack to the lowest part of your oven and preheat the oven to 350ºF. Generously butter a 9-inch springform pan. Wrap the bottom of the pan in two sheets of aluminum foil (if you are doing the water bath method).

- To make the crust: Place the crackers in the bowl of a food processor and pulse until they are finely ground. Transfer to a bowl and stir in the melted butter and sugar (if using) until combined.

- Pour the crumbs into the prepared pan, using the bottom of a glass to gently press the crumbs against the bottom and up the sides of the pan.

- To make the filling: In the bowl of a stand mixer fitted with the paddle attachment, combine the cream cheese and sugar until smooth. With the mixer on low speed, add the milk, sour cream, and vanilla. Scrape down the sides of the bowl and with the mixer on low speed, add the eggs one at a time.

- Add the sifted flour and stir with a spatula. Scrape down the sides of the bowl and pour the filling over the crust in the pan (see tip for water bath instructions). Bake for 1 hour. When the time is up, turn off the oven, crack the door, and leave the cheesecake inside to cool and set for 4 to 5 hours, then refrigerate it overnight.

- Slice and serve with Roasted Maple Strawberry Sauce over the top.

Roasted Maple Strawberry Sauce

INGREDIENTS:

1 pound strawberries, hulled and halved

1 teaspoon lemon zest

2 tablespoons fresh lemon juice, strained

2 tablespoons pure maple syrup

Pinch of sea salt

½ teaspoon pure vanilla extract

Whether drizzled warm over ice cream, or chilled and served with cheesecake, this maple strawberry sauce is amazing and incredibly versatile. There's no need to ever buy a sauce like this in a store—it's so easy to make at home!

This strawberry sauce is excellent slightly warm and spooned over Vanilla Bean Ice Cream (page 269) or Lazy Weekend Yeasted Waffles (page 64), or chill and serve over slices of Homemade New York-Style Cheesecake (page 279).

MAKES 1½ CUPS • TOTAL TIME: 35 MINUTES

DIRECTIONS:

- Preheat the oven to 400°F.

- Mix the strawberries, lemon zest and juice, maple syrup, and salt in a 2-quart baking dish. Roast for 15 minutes. Pull them out and give them a quick stir with a spoon before roasting for 10 minutes more.

- Remove and let the strawberries cool for 15 to 20 minutes before serving warm.

SIMPLY SCRATCH TIP

Feel free to switch things up! Use blueberries or a combination of other berries.

Caramelized Bananas with Spiced Coconut Milk & Granola

This is somewhat of a fancy nod to a "dessert" my mom would make me as a kid. I use air-quotes because, let's be real, bananas in milk with a sprinkle of sugar is hardly what a kid (or any grown-up) would call dessert. But I absolutely loved it. However, THIS dessert is totally all that and a bag of chips. The coconut milk is spiced up with fresh ginger, a cinnamon stick, and fresh nutmeg. Bananas are caramelized in brown sugar *and* butter. And all this happens while a simple 5-minute granola is toasting in the oven. Try this with a sprinkle of toasted coconut on top!

SERVES 4 • TOTAL TIME: 35 MINUTES

DIRECTIONS:

- To make the granola: Preheat the oven to 325ºF.

- In a large bowl, combine the oats and walnuts.

- In a small saucepan, melt the butter. Remove from the heat and add the honey, brown sugar, vanilla, cinnamon, and salt. Stir until combined and pour over the oats and nuts. Toss until combined, spread onto a rimmed baking sheet, and bake for 10 to 15 minutes. The granola will crisp up more as it cools.

- Meanwhile, to make the spiced coconut milk: With the bottom of your knife handle, smash the ginger coins.

- In a medium saucepan, combine the coconut milk, ginger, and cinnamon stick; bring to a gentle simmer over medium to medium-low heat and cook for 10 minutes.

- Remove from the heat and stir in the maple syrup, vanilla, and nutmeg. Let steep for 5 minutes before pouring through a mesh strainer into a large liquid measuring cup or bowl. Chill until ready to serve.

INGREDIENTS:

FOR THE GRANOLA:

1 cup old-fashioned oats

¼ cup chopped walnuts

1 tablespoon unsalted butter

2 tablespoons honey

1 tablespoon dark brown sugar

¼ teaspoon pure vanilla extract

¼ teaspoon ground cinnamon

Pinch of kosher salt

FOR THE SPICED COCONUT MILK:

1 (2-inch) piece fresh ginger, peeled and sliced into 4 thick coins

1 cup light coconut milk

1 cinnamon stick

1 tablespoon pure maple syrup

¼ teaspoon pure vanilla extract

⅛ teaspoon freshly grated nutmeg

FOR THE CARAMELIZED BANANAS:

3 tablespoons unsalted butter

3 tablespoons dark brown sugar

Pinch of kosher salt

4 small slightly underripe bananas, sliced ½ inch thick (about 24 slices)

- To make the caramelized bananas: Heat a 12-inch nonstick skillet over medium heat; add the butter, brown sugar, and salt and stir until the brown sugar has dissolved. Once bubbling, add the sliced bananas, arranging them in an even layer, and let them cook untouched for 2 to 3 minutes, or until they turn a deep golden color on the bottom. Flip and repeat until the bananas are caramelized and the sugar-butter mixture has thickened. Spoon the bubbling brown sugar butter over the top of the bananas once you have flipped them.

- Divide the chilled coconut milk among six small bowls, add 4 to 5 caramelized banana slices to each bowl, and top with some of the granola.

Mississippi Mud Pie
(But Actually Texas Sheet Cake)

If there's one misleading recipe title in this cookbook, this is it. My whole life, I've known this dessert as Mississippi Mud Pie, but in reality, it's not. Have I confused you yet? The real Mississippi Mud Pie is an *actual* pie, and the version I'd been eating my whole life is really known as Texas Sheet Cake. It wasn't until very recently that I discovered the difference, and soon after, the realization sank in that I'd been lied to my whole childhood. I'm kidding (sort of). When I asked my mom, she said the name was fun and it just sort of stuck. I don't know about you, but I'm now questioning everything she's ever told me. Really.

Either way, this Mississippi-Mud-Pie-that's-really-Texas-Sheet-Cake recipe holds fond memories for me. I remember pulling up our rusty-brown-colored stepstool to the kitchen counter and watching my mom pour warm walnut-studded frosting over the cake when it was fresh from the oven. It's sweet and chocolaty, and the frosting is divine.

SERVES 20 • TOTAL TIME: 35 TO 40 MINUTES

DIRECTIONS:

- To make the cake: Preheat the oven to 375°F. Butter a rimmed 18 by 13-inch sheet pan and line it with parchment paper.

- In a saucepan, combine the butter, cocoa powder, and 1 cup water. Bring to a boil, stirring often, then remove from the heat and let cool.

- In a medium bowl, whisk together the flour, sugar, baking soda, and salt to combine.

- In the bowl of a mixer fitted with the paddle attachment, beat together the eggs, buttermilk, vinegar, and vanilla until combined. Add the dry ingredients along with the cooled

INGREDIENTS:

FOR THE CAKE:

1 cup (2 sticks) unsalted butter, plus 1 tablespoon for the pan

¼ cup unsweetened cocoa powder

2 cups unbleached all-purpose flour

2 cups granulated sugar

1 teaspoon baking soda

½ teaspoon kosher salt

2 large eggs

½ cup buttermilk

1 teaspoon distilled white vinegar

1 teaspoon pure vanilla extract

FOR THE FROSTING:

8 tablespoons (1 stick) unsalted butter

¼ cup unsweetened cocoa powder

6 tablespoons whole milk

4 cups powdered sugar

1 teaspoon pure vanilla extract

½ cup chopped walnuts

cocoa-butter mixture. Blend until smooth and pour onto the prepared baking sheet.

- Bake for 20 minutes, or until a cake tester inserted into the center comes out clean.

TO MAKE THE FROSTING

- In a small saucepan, combine the butter, cocoa powder, and milk. Heat over low heat until the butter has melted. Stir in the powdered sugar, vanilla, and walnuts until smooth.

- Pour the frosting over the center of the cake when it's fresh from the oven. Move quickly and spread the frosting evenly over the cake with a spatula. Let the cake cool before cutting it into squares and serving.

SIMPLY SCRATCH TIP

Since this recipe yields such a large cake, it's great for serving a crowd.

Olive Oil Zucchini Bread

INGREDIENTS:

2 cups unbleached all-purpose flour, plus more for dusting

3 tablespoons ground cinnamon

2 teaspoons baking soda

¼ teaspoon baking powder

1 teaspoon kosher salt

3 large eggs

2 cups sugar

½ cup unsweetened applesauce

½ cup good-quality olive oil

1 tablespoon pure vanilla extract

2 generous cups grated zucchini

This zucchini bread recipe was one of the earliest recipes I shared on my blog. It's now buried under hundreds of recipes, but it's still one of my all-time favorites. It makes two loaves, so you can keep one and give away the other to a friend or neighbor. Or wrap the extra loaf in plastic wrap and heavy aluminum foil once it's cooled and store it in the freezer for another day.

This flavorful and moist zucchini bread is just begging to be toasted and buttered.

MAKES 2 LOAVES • TOTAL TIME: 1 HOUR

DIRECTIONS:

- Preheat the oven to 350ºF. Butter two 9 by 5-inch loaf pans and line them with parchment (or butter and flour them, omitting the parchment paper).

- In a large bowl, sift together the flour, cinnamon, baking soda, and baking powder. Add the salt and set aside.

- In a separate bowl, whisk together the eggs, sugar, applesauce, oil, and vanilla. Add the grated zucchini. Pour the wet mixture into the bowl with the flour ingredients, stir until just incorporated, and divide the batter between the two prepared pans (about 2½ cups per pan).

- Bake for 40 to 45 minutes, or until a tester inserted into the center comes out with a few crumbs still attached.

- Let cool completely in the pans before removing and slicing.

Winter Apple & Pear Shortcakes

My all-time favorite summertime dessert is strawberry short-cakes. I make them just about every other weekend. Extra strawberries and extra whipped cream, please!

So I thought, *Why not create a winter version, since strawber-ries are out of season when it's cold outside?* And it clicked: I could use apples and pears! Then I came up with these tender whole wheat shortcakes and a rum-spiked whipped cream. Be-cause in winter, everything should be rum-spiked. End of story.

Pull out the fuzzy slippers and board games—it's about to get real cozy!

MAKES 8 SHORTCAKES • TOTAL TIME: 30 TO 40 MINUTES

DIRECTIONS:

- To make the shortcakes: Preheat the oven to 425°F. Line a rimmed baking sheet with parchment paper or a silicone baking mat.

- In a large bowl, whisk together the flours, sugar, baking pow-der, baking soda, and salt. Use a pastry cutter to cut and blend the butter into the dry ingredients.

- In a separate bowl, combine the 1/3 cup buttermilk, egg, and vanilla. Add the egg mixture to the flour mixture, stirring un-til a flaky dough comes together.

- Turn the dough out onto a lightly floured surface. Use a roll-ing pin to roll out the dough to 3/4 inch thick and use a 3-inch biscuit cutter to stamp out 8 shortcakes. Transfer the short-cakes to the prepared baking sheet. Brush the tops with the remaining 1 tablespoon buttermilk and sprinkle with turbi-nado sugar. Bake for 12 to 14 minutes, or until golden.

- To make the filling: In a large bowl, combine the apples, pears, lemon juice, brown sugar, cinnamon, nutmeg, ginger, cornstarch, and salt. Melt the butter in a 12-inch skillet over medium heat, add the apple and pear mixture plus 1/4 cup of

INGREDIENTS:

FOR THE SHORTCAKES:

1 1/4 cups unbleached all-purpose flour, plus more for dusting

3/4 cup whole wheat flour

3 tablespoons light brown sugar

2 teaspoons baking powder

1/2 teaspoon baking soda

1/2 teaspoon kosher salt

4 tablespoons cold unsalted butter

1/3 cup plus 1 tablespoon buttermilk

1 large egg, lightly beaten

1 teaspoon pure vanilla extract

Turbinado sugar

FOR THE FILLING:

2 Honeycrisp apples, unpeeled, cored and diced (about 4 cups)

2 Bosc pears, unpeeled, cored and diced (about 4 cups)

1 tablespoon fresh lemon juice

1/2 cup packed light brown sugar

3/4 teaspoon ground cinnamon

1/8 teaspoon freshly grated nutmeg

1/4 teaspoon ground ginger

2 tablespoons cornstarch

1/4 teaspoon kosher salt

2 tablespoons unsalted butter

1/2 teaspoon pure vanilla extract

water, and cook until the fruit is tender, 25 to 30 minutes. Add more water if the liquids have thickened too quickly. (The cooking time may vary depending on how ripe the pears are.)

- Once the fruit is tender and the liquids have thickened, remove from the heat and stir in the vanilla. Let cool slightly.

- While the fruit cools down, prepare the Rum Whipped Cream (page 293). Keep refrigerated until you are ready to serve.

- To serve, slice the warm shortcakes in half, top the bottom half with a large spoonful of warm apple and pear filling, and spoon on a dollop of rum whipped cream. Add the shortcake top and spoon on more filling and whipped cream. Serve immediately.

Whipped Cream, Three Ways

A tub of Cool Whip or a can of Reddi-wip never graced my childhood fridge. We always, ALWAYS had whipped cream from scratch. Every holiday, birthday, you name it, dessert wasn't ready until my mom pulled the bowl and beaters out of the freezer and made whipped cream. It took no time—less than 5 minutes—and the texture and taste were incomparable.

As you probably guessed, I, too, make my own whipped cream. There's nothing like cinnamon whipped cream in a mug of hot cocoa, or rum-spiked whip with my Winter Apple & Pear Shortcakes (page 291), and both my daughters adore chocolate whipped cream for dipping strawberries in . . . and everything in between.

MAKES 2 CUPS • TOTAL TIME: 25 MINUTES (INCLUDES BOWL/ BEATER CHILLING)

DIRECTIONS:

- Chill a glass or metal bowl and beater attachments for 20 to 30 minutes in the freezer before you begin.

- Place the cream in the chilled bowl and beat on low speed until the cream has thickened slightly. Add the powdered sugar, vanilla, and any other ingredients (see Fun Variations below) and continue to mix, increasing the speed to medium, until thick. Use immediately or cover and refrigerate until ready to serve. If you are refrigerating, you may need to mix it again when you are ready to use it to fluff the settled whipped cream.

FUN VARIATIONS:

- Cinnamon Whipped Cream: Add ½ teaspoon ground cinnamon.

- Chocolate Whipped Cream: Add 2½ tablespoons unsweetened cocoa powder. (Make a half hour in advance so the cocoa powder has a chance to soften in the cream.)

- Rum Whipped Cream: Add 2 tablespoons dark rum.

INGREDIENTS:

1 cup cold heavy cream

2 tablespoons powdered sugar, sifted

½ teaspoon pure vanilla extract

Rhubarb Hand Pies

I've loved rhubarb for as long as I can remember. We had a large rhubarb plant in our huge garden along the side of my childhood home. Every spring, my mom would make the BEST rhubarb pie. This recipe is no exception. It's simple and classic, and I put it into a nifty handheld package for your convenience. You're welcome.

MAKES 6 PIES • TOTAL TIME: ABOUT 2 HOURS

DIRECTIONS:

- Combine the rhubarb, brown sugar, lemon zest and juice, ginger, salt, and 1/4 cup water in a medium saucepan. Bring to a boil over high heat, then reduce the heat to medium-low and simmer for 12 to 15 minutes, or until the rhubarb mixture is thick. Remove from the heat, stir in the vanilla then pour into a heat-safe bowl to cool completely. (I set the bowl in a second, larger bowl filled with ice to speed this process along.)

- Preheat the oven to 400ºF. In a small bowl, combine the beaten egg with 1 tablespoon water to make an egg wash.

- Roll out one disc of dough to 1/8 inch thick. Use a 6-inch biscuit cutter to stamp out 3 circles. Brush the outer edges with a little egg wash before spooning 2 tablespoons of the cooled rhubarb mixture onto one half of each circle. Fold the unfilled side over the filling and crimp the edges with a fork. Brush the tops of each pie with more of the egg wash. With a sharp knife, make slits in the center for ventilation and sprinkle each pie with 1/2 teaspoon of turbinado sugar. Refrigerate. Repeat with the second disc of pie dough and remaining filling.

- Bake for 15 to 18 minutes or until the crust is golden and the filling is bubbling. Let the pies cool on the baking sheet for 10 minutes before transferring them to a wire rack.

INGREDIENTS:

¾ pound fresh rhubarb, trimmed and cut into ½-inch pieces

⅓ cup packed dark brown sugar

1 teaspoon lemon zest

1 teaspoon fresh lemon juice

¼ teaspoon ground ginger

¼ teaspoon kosher salt

1 teaspoon pure vanilla extract

1 recipe All-Purpose Pie Crust (2 discs; page 49)

1 large egg, beaten

Turbinado sugar

Glazed Butter Rum Cake

This cake. It's everything I love wrapped into one beautiful Bundt-tastic beauty. And the sprinkling of toasted chopped pecans sends it into heavenly oblivion.

What I love most about this cake is the glaze. It's just a light glaze made up of a simple syrup, rum, butter, and vanilla. It truly is something magical (and ridiculously simple).

MAKES 1 BUNDT CAKE, TO SERVE ABOUT 10 • TOTAL TIME: 2 HOURS

DIRECTIONS:

- To make the cake: Preheat the oven to 325°F. Generously butter and lightly flour a 10-cup Bundt pan. Tap the pan to remove any excess flour.

- In a medium bowl, whisk together the flour, baking powder, baking soda, and salt. Set aside.

- In the bowl of a stand mixer fitted with the paddle attachment, beat together the butter and sugar on medium-low speed until light, fluffy, and pale in color. With the mixer on low, gradually add the eggs one at a time, mixing after each addition.

- Combine the buttermilk, rum, and vanilla. Alternate adding the flour mixture and the buttermilk mixture, starting and ending with the flour mixture, and mix until just combined. Do not overmix.

- Spoon the batter into the prepared pan and bake on the center rack for 1 hour, or until a tester inserted into the center comes out with only a few crumbs.

- To make the glaze: Five minutes before the cake is finished baking, in a medium saucepan, combine the sugar and ½ cup water and heat until the sugar has dissolved. Remove and stir in the rum, butter, and vanilla.

INGREDIENTS:

FOR THE CAKE

1 cup (2 sticks) unsalted butter, at room temperature, plus more for the pan

3 cups unbleached all-purpose flour, plus more for the pan

1 teaspoon baking powder

1 teaspoon baking soda

1 teaspoon kosher salt

2 cups sugar

4 large eggs, at room temperature

½ cup buttermilk, at room temperature

½ cup dark rum

2 teaspoons pure vanilla extract

FOR THE GLAZE:

1 cup sugar

2 tablespoons dark rum

2 tablespoons unsalted butter

1 teaspoon pure vanilla extract

½ cup chopped pecans, toasted

- With the cake still in the pan, use a skewer to poke holes in the warm cake and spoon half the glaze over the top.

- Let the cake cool for 25 to 30 minutes before carefully inverting it onto a wire rack.

- Once completely cooled, reheat the glaze and use a pastry brush to brush the glaze over the cake until no glaze remains. Sprinkle with the pecans.

- Let the glaze harden before cutting and serving.

SIMPLY SCRATCH TIP

The best method I've found to get the cake to slide right out of the Bundt pan is to give the pan a good coating with butter and a dusting of flour before pouring in the batter. I put 1½ tablespoons butter into a clean, dry pan and use a paper towel to smear it into all the nooks and crannies. Then I add 1 tablespoon flour and tip the pan until it has a light coating (tap out any excess). I've tried nonstick sprays, and they can pool in the bottom of the pan and absorb the flour, which gives the finished cake flour/spray blotches. So not pretty.

Pecan Toffee Oatmeal Cookies

Honestly, I've always been a cookie person. It could be eight p.m., but if I'm craving cookies suddenly, I'll stop what I'm doing and whip up a batch. Growing up, cookies were one homemade treat that I'd make for myself. I'd pull out my mom's 1970-something (and now considered vintage) brown Mixmaster and bust out some serious cookies.

Even though these cookies look like unassuming oatmeal cookies, they actually taste quite the opposite. When pecans, toffee, and oatmeal are involved, you can pretty much assume greatness will follow. These treats don't need to be gussied up with chocolate chips or raisins. But a glass of milk or coffee on the side wouldn't be too shabby of an idea.

MAKES 3 DOZEN • TOTAL TIME: 1 HOUR

DIRECTIONS:

- Preheat the oven to 350ºF. Line two rimmed baking sheets with parchment paper or silicone liners.

- In a medium bowl, combine the flour, baking soda, cinnamon, and salt and set aside.

- In the bowl of a stand mixer fitted with the paddle attachment, cream together the butter and both sugars until light and fluffy, about 2 minutes. Add the vanilla. Add the eggs one at a time, mixing and scraping down the sides of the bowl after adding each egg. Gradually add the flour mixture until just combined.

- With the mixer on low, stir in the oats, pecans, and toffee bits.

- Using a 2-tablespoon scoop, measure out the cookie dough onto the prepared baking sheets, spacing them 1/2 inch apart. Bake for 10 to 12 minutes, rotating the baking sheets halfway during bake time for even baking.

INGREDIENTS

1 ½ cups unbleached all-purpose flour

1 teaspoon baking soda

¾ teaspoon ground cinnamon

¾ teaspoon kosher salt

1 cup (2 sticks) unsalted butter

1 cup packed dark brown sugar

½ cup granulated sugar

1 teaspoon pure vanilla extract

2 large eggs

3 cups old-fashioned oats

¾ cup chopped pecans, toasted

1 cup toffee pieces (I use Heath Bits'o Brickle)

- Let cool on the baking sheets for 5 minutes before using a spatula to transfer to a wire rack. Repeat with the remaining dough.

- These cookies are extra delicious if they are served when still warm.

Fresh Cherry Pie with Walnut-Thyme Crumb

I live in the "mitten" state, so cherries are abundant in the summer months. Haileigh, my oldest, and I will sit on the front porch with a colander of sweet dark cherries and polish them off in no time flat. But in a pie is where I love them best.

If you don't own a cherry pitter, you don't have to run out of the house to buy one. I still don't own one. I use the blunt end of a wooden skewer to push the pit out. Although it is more time consuming, and your hands will look like a crime scene, it does work!

The combination of both sweet and tart cherries, paired with the thyme crumble, is an out-of-this-world match made in pie heaven.

SERVES 8 • TOTAL TIME: 1 HOUR 30 MINUTES

DIRECTIONS:

- Preheat the oven to 400°F.

- Roll the dough out to fit a 9-inch pie plate. Fold and crimp the edges, then refrigerate until ready to fill.

- To make the filling: In a large bowl, combine the cherries and sugar. Stir and let sit for 5 minutes. Add the cornstarch, salt, lemon juice, and vanilla and stir to combine. Pour the filling into the chilled pie crust and bake on the center rack for 25 minutes.

- Meanwhile, to make the topping: In a medium bowl, combine the flours, sugar, walnuts, thyme, and salt. Pour in the butter and with a rubber spatula, stir to combine. Use your fingers to form crumbles.

INGREDIENTS:

1 recipe All-Purpose Pie Crust (1 disc; page 49)

FOR THE FILLING:

3 cups fresh dark sweet cherries, pitted

2 cups fresh tart cherries, pitted

½ cup sugar

2 tablespoons cornstarch

⅛ teaspoon kosher salt

2 teaspoons fresh lemon juice

¾ teaspoon pure vanilla extract

FOR THE CRUMB TOPPING:

½ cup unbleached all-purpose flour

¼ cup whole wheat flour

½ cup granulated sugar

½ cup finely chopped walnuts

½ teaspoon chopped fresh thyme leaves

¼ teaspoon kosher salt

6 tablespoons unsalted butter, melted

- After the pie has baked for 25 minutes, remove it from the oven and top with the crumb mixture. Bake for 25 minutes more, or until the crust is golden and the filling is bubbling.

- Let cool for 30 minutes before slicing and serving.

SIMPLY SCRATCH TIP

If using frozen cherries, do not thaw prior to making the pie filling and up the cornstarch by at least a tablespoon or two.

Grilled Vanilla Cardamom Pound Cake with Caramelized Pineapple

Grilled cake: it's a thing, you guys! Grilling adds another textural dimension and unexpected flavor to this cardamom-spiced pound cake. It adds a "WOW" factor that is sure to impress.

Topped with pineapple that has been caramelized in brown sugar and butter, and homemade cinnamon whipped cream (or hey, RUM-spiked is another option!), after one bite you'll be transported to the beach of some tropical island surrounded by palm trees and turquoise waters. Or maybe that's just me.

MAKES 1 LOAF, TO SERVE ABOUT 8 • TOTAL TIME: 2 HOURS
30 MINUTES

DIRECTIONS:

- Preheat the oven to 350°F. Butter and sugar an 8 by 5-inch loaf pan.

- To make the pound cake: In a large bowl, sift together the flour, baking powder, baking soda, salt, and cardamom. Set aside.

- In a small bowl, combine the milk, sour cream, and vanilla.

- In the bowl of a stand mixer fitted with the paddle attachment, cream the butter and granulated sugar on medium-low speed for 2 to 3 minutes, or until light and fluffy. With the mixer on low, add the eggs one at a time, mixing after each egg. Add the flour mixture to the batter, alternating with the milk mixture and beginning and ending with the flour.

- Pour the batter into the prepared loaf pan. With a spatula, smooth out the top. Bake for 50 to 55 minutes, or until a cake tester inserted into the center comes out clean. Let cool in the pan for 10 minutes before running a knife around the

INGREDIENTS:

½ tablespoon unsalted butter

1 tablespoon granulated sugar

FOR THE POUND CAKE:

1½ cups unbleached all-purpose flour

¼ teaspoon baking powder

¼ teaspoon baking soda

½ teaspoon kosher salt

¾ teaspoon ground cardamom

¼ cup plus 2 tablespoons whole milk, at room temperature

¼ cup sour cream, at room temperature

1 teaspoon pure vanilla extract

8 tablespoons (1 stick) unsalted butter, at room temperature

1 cup granulated sugar

2 large eggs, at room temperature

FOR THE CARAMELIZED PINEAPPLE:

4 tablespoons unsalted butter

⅓ cup packed light or dark brown sugar

3 cups diced fresh pineapple

Melted butter, for grilling

Cinnamon Whipped Cream (see page 293), for serving

edges and removing the cake from the pan. Place the cake on a wire rack and let cool completely.

- Once it's cool, the pound cake can be wrapped tightly in plastic wrap and stored in the refrigerator until you are ready to serve it.

- To make the caramelized pineapple: In a 10-inch saucepan, melt the butter and brown sugar. Add the pineapple, raise the heat to medium-high, and cook, basting it in the butter-sugar mixture until caramelized, 12 to 15 minutes.

- Heat a grill pan over medium-high heat. Slice the pound cake into 1/2-inch slices and brush with melted butter. Grill for 1 to 3 minutes per side.

- Top the grilled pound cake slices with a spoonful of caramelized pineapple and a dollop of cinnamon whipped cream.

Watermelon Granita

Who likes to turn on the oven in the summer? Not me. I prefer to grill outdoors and have a cool, refreshing dessert. A granita is the perfect light summertime dessert. Fresh watermelon, lime juice, and sugar are all you need to make this icy, delicious treat.

SERVES 8 OR MORE • TOTAL TIME: 10 MINUTES PLUS 2 HOURS

INGREDIENTS:

¼ cup fresh lime juice

¼ cup sugar

8 cups cubed seedless watermelon

DIRECTIONS:

- Place a metal 8 by 8-inch pan in the freezer.

- In a small saucepan, heat the lime juice and sugar over medium heat, stirring until the sugar has dissolved. Remove from the heat and let cool.

- Working in batches, in a high-powered blender or the bowl of a food processor, pulse the watermelon until ultra-smooth. Add the lime simple syrup and pulse to combine.

- Pour the watermelon puree into the chilled pan and freeze for 20 to 30 minutes. Use a fork to scrape any icy parts into the center and return the granita to the freezer for 20 minutes more. Continue scraping the watermelon every 20 minutes or so until it's completely frozen and slushy, about 2 hours total.

- Serve in chilled bowls.

Index

Page numbers in *italics* indicate photographs.